*This collection of essays was
awarded the Di Castagnola Prize
of the Poetry Society of America*

Conviction's Net
of Branches

*Essays on
the Objectivist Poets
and Poetry*

Michael Heller

Southern Illinois University Press
Carbondale and Edwardsville

Permission to quote from copyrighted works
appears on pp. xiii–xiv.

Copyright © 1985 by the Board of Trustees,
Southern Illinois University
All rights reserved
Printed in the United States of America
Edited by Yvonne Dunnenberger
Designed by Quentin Fiore
Production supervised by Kathleen Giencke

Library of Congress Cataloging in Publication Data

Heller, Michael, 1937–
  Conviction's net of branches.

  Bibliography: p.
  Includes index.
    1. American poetry—20th century—History and
criticism—Addresses, essays, lectures. 2. Poetics—
Addresses, essays, lectures. I. Title. II. Title:
Objectivist poets and poetry.
PS324.H4 1985   811'.52'09   84-1339
ISBN 0-8093-1176-3
ISBN 0-8093-1188-7 (pbk.)

88 87 86 85   4 3 2 1

This Book is for Armand and Hugh, and for Cid

Contents

Preface

An Objective: (Optics)—The lens bringing rays from an object to a focus. That which is aimed at. (Use extended to poetry)—Desire for what is objectively perfect, inextricably the direction of historic and contemporary particulars.

— Louis Zukofsky, An "Objectivists" Anthology[1]

Use extended to poetry: the word "Objectivist" referring to a group of poets gathered under the editorial hand of Louis Zukofsky for Harriet Monroe's *Poetry* magazine in 1931, the space in the magazine having been won through the tutelary insistences applied to Miss Monroe by Ezra Pound. Included were twenty poets. The name, as Zukofsky recounts in an interview some forty years later: "Well, she (Harriet Monroe) told me, 'You must have a movement.'"[2] And though at first resistant, Zukofsky finally assented, essentially coining the name by labeling his selections "objectivist." Part of Zukofsky's assent also involved writing a covering essay entitled "An Objective," which, though meant to explain or define the reasons behind his choices, was ultimately to become one of the major statements of a "poetics" of the twentieth century, a document which now looms as nearly equal in force to Pound's Imagist manifestos or Charles Olson's "Projective Verse." This essay and the poems from the magazine were reprinted in the following year, 1932, by TO Press (run by Zukofsky and George Oppen) under the title *An "Objectivists" Anthology.*

Use extended to poetry: The historical moment in poetry, however, out of which the Objectivist poets emerged was by no means a simple function of Zukofsky's personal taste and Monroe's pressure for a name. It was rather but one event in a cluster of events which followed on the accomplishments of the earlier modernists, Pound, Joyce, Eliot and another half-dozen or so figures in the visual arts and music, whose work and thought permeated every creative field of the times. In her memoir *Meaning A Life*, Mary Oppen, the wife of George Oppen, describes the couple's arrival in New York in the late twenties where they were surrounded by young people united in breaking with old traditions, who "had the conviction that the works of artists and writers had to be new or there was no point in the effort."[3] In poetry, Pound's banner "Make it new" seemed to wave from the end of a broom which was sweeping the old Victorian pomposity and false optimism out of the very house of creation. At the same time, it gave young poets such as the Objectivists a warrant not only to question but, perhaps most importantly, to sanction what was new, experimental, at odds with the worn-out conventions of nineteenth-century verse.

Yet for the Objectivist, as for many other poets of the time, this era of experimentation was problematic: the overthrow of the older poetic modalities was not only liberating but it also led the poet into a *terra incognita*. For what fell on the poet's newly unburdened shoulders was the question of—or to be more precise—the responsibility of form. The seeming bankruptcy of the older conventions (not for their time, but for the modernist era) placed the poet under a peculiar tension, presenting him or her with a conscious sense of uncertainty concerning the relations between form, expression, and communication. Put simply, the new question which the example of modernism asked was: what is recognizably poetry? This was not just a reader's question but one which the poet faced, having, on the one hand, a concrete "something" to express and, on the other hand, a plentitude of new means at his or her disposal.

The thirties, the formative years of the Objectivists, can be seen as a great shaking-out of various means to resolve these tensions aroused by the modernist overthrow. Among the poets, this led to various consolidations and groupings based on like-mindedness or mutual defense, or it led to ideological quarrels which fed not only on poetic issues but on the immense political ferment generated by the Depression, the New Deal, and the rise of Fascism.

In such a climate, a name or label, however reluctantly given, becomes, if not a definition, a reference point, a locus of shared engagements. It also has the possibility of becoming a micro-instant of what Pound once thought civilization consisted of: a group of people *who know* arguing and discussing.

Time, death, literary diversity, and disagreement peeled away this label that was nearly no label from one after another of the poets in the anthology. With a few poets, however, those included in this study, the name Objectivist stuck. It seemed to have adhered, *ex post facto*, so to speak, to these poets, who were aligned, accidentally and coincidentally, by friendship, correspondence, proximity*, publishing ventures (TO Press), and a sharing of broad mutual interests, such as the urban experience, politics, the influence and example of Pound and Williams (this group's "older generation"), and possibly the solitariness each may have felt was his or her portion, working as they did in mutual obscurity and distance from the academy and its enthusiasms and concerns.

Despite the circumstances by which these poets were grouped and named, and despite the wide differences readily perceivable in their work, an original and forceful commonality among them, less articulated than intuited, can be dis-

---

*In the case of Oppen, Reznikoff and Zukofsky, this was mainly New York and the New Jersey of William Carlos Williams.

cerned, which has caused them to be regarded as a group by both critics and poets. This commonality, which I see as of contemporary significance and deeply related to the meaning and importance of the poet's role in the world and to poetic craft, is decidedly not accidental, as I hope this study will demonstrate. Indeed, one of my intentions here will be to fill out, in critical shorthand, the space opened by Hugh Kenner's comment on the Objectivists in *The Pound Era*: "(Objectivist) history is still unwritten."[4] My purpose here is, first, to show the particular distinctiveness of the Objectivists and the qualities of the particular space they inhabit in the topography of American poetry.* Secondly, and perhaps more importantly, I want to present "first word" and not "last word" readings of their works, not only as aspects of an "Objectivist" tradition but as valuable and meaningful poetry, significant human documentation to be studied for what it can tell us about our lives and our times.

*I have not included a discussion of the English poet Basil Bunting, who is often linked with these poets, since my subject here is American poetry. It can be argued that Bunting, as well as some other Objectivist-influenced poets in England, represents another line of development worthy of study by some English critic.

Acknowledgments

I would like to thank Gerard Grealish for his help in compiling the Objectivist bibliography. I am very much in his debt. I would also like to thank Yvonne Dunnenberger of Southern Illinois University Press for her inestimable help in going over the manuscript and suggesting many useful felicities concerning the text.

My thanks to the Poetry Society of America. That organization's Alice Fay Di Castagnola award was both a financial and emotional spur toward completing this work.

To George and Mary Oppen and to Carl and Leah Rakosi for nearly two decades of art, high and low talk and generosity, my deepest gratitude.

To Ernie Raia, who set me on my way, my fondest regards.

Permissions from the following publishers are gratefully acknowledged:

Black Sparrow Press: *Primitive* by George Oppen, Copyright ©; *Ex Cranium, Night* by Carl Rakosi, Copyright ©; *The Complete Poems, Volumes I and II* by Charles Reznikoff, Copyright ©

New Directions: George Oppen, *Collected Poems of George Op-*

Parts of the essays included in this collection have been previously published in the following journals:

"Carl Rakosi: Poetry of the Lived World," *Montemora #8.*

"I've Seen It There," a review of Lorine Niedecker's Poetry, *The Nation*, April 13, 1970. Copyright © 1970 by *Nation* magazine, The Nation Associates, Inc.

"The Objectivists: Some Discrete Speculations," *The Ohio Review*, no. 26.

"The Poetry of Louis Zukofsky: To Draw Speech," *Origin*, The National Poetry Foundation.

"Review of George Oppen," *The American Poetry Review*, vol. 4, no. 2.

"Some Reflections and Extensions: Zukofsky's Poetics," *Maps* 5.

Conviction's Net
of Branches

1 The Objectivists:
Some Discrete Speculations

Without fanfare and in spite of a curious kind of neglect, the Objectivist poets (Oppen, Rakosi, Reznikoff and Zukofsky) continue to attract, to insinuate themselves into the American body poetic, to acquire a committed readership. There has been a recent blush of auspiciousness: George Oppen's *Collected Poems* (New Directions), Black Sparrow's ongoing publication of Reznikoff's complete prose, plays and poetry, and, in addition, Carl Rakosi's large collection of poems, *Ex Cranium, Night*. There has always been an English interest in the Objectivists, and now a European point of view is being expressed. This latter is suggestive. The French critic and translator, Serge Fauchereau, in a recent issue of *Ironwood*, summarizes: "Objectivism must be considered as the first deliberately American movement. . . . [It] reappears not only as a historically important movement, but also as the only one to have left something."[1]

These brief notes attempt to explore what that "something" is.

Modern American poetry of whatever stripe and caliber can be examined under the aspect of vision, not vision with a capital V, but vision as the poet's imagining (for want of a better word) pictorialized. Vision here would mean using language as a painter might use paint, to create a structure of relations, a spatio-linguistic object (the contemporary poem), embodied in and being conditioned by thought and by the traditional means of poetry such as meter, stress, diction and tone. To borrow from Wittgenstein, most poetry written today shows rather than states its rhetoric (its propositions?). In the twentieth century, the pivotal factors have been Imagism, Eliot's objective correlative and the ideogrammatic method, but one can look for beginnings as far back as Whitman's injunction in "Starting From Paumanouk":

> Was somebody asking to see the soul?
> See, your own shape and countenance, persons,
> substances, beasts, the trees, the running rivers,
> the rocks and sands.[2]

If today, that "soul" all too easily translates into the Self, imperial or otherwise, but mainly secular, the "See" of the poem, if we read Whitman right, has about it moral and philosophical pressure. This pressure, mostly underplayed in Whitman criticism, would define him less the poet of an untrammeled self and more the poet caught up in what I think is a modern recognition, a recognition which lies at the core of what the Objectivists are up to.

Zukofsky, perhaps with Imagism rather than Whitman in particular on his mind, reformulated "Paumanouk" in the 1931 Objectivist Anthology issue of *Poetry* magazine:

> In sincerity shapes appear concomitants of word combinations, precursors of (if there is to be continuance) completed sound or structure, melody or form. Writing occurs which is the detail, not mirage of seeing, of thinking with things as they exist ...[3]

Although shorn of soul-dust and a pantheism which science (our newer mythology) has consigned to ids and quarks, this statement is not merely technical; it is made into a moral charge by the operative phrase "in sincerity." Pointed back at the Imagists, it was an admonishment meant to steer an erring poetry that had once been a good thing (Imagism, we recall, abolished numerous "useless" verse conventions) back on course. It was not so much technique as it was honor code. George Oppen, whose work was printed in that 1931 Objectivist Anthology, put it this way in a letter to Fauchereau (reprinted in *Ironwood*):

> The image for the sake of the poet, not for the sake of the reader. The image as a test of sincerity, as against: "the sun rose like a red-faced farmer leaning over a fence", which last is a picture intended for the delectation of the reader who may be imagined to admire the quaintness and ingenuity of the poet, but can scarcely have been a part of the poet's attempt to find himself in the world—unless perhaps to find himself as a charming conversationalist.[4]

Oppen, who should have been a little red-faced himself, since the poem alluded to above, Hulme's *Autumn*, is about the moon, not the sun, was echoing one of Pound's early critique demands of the movement: "The point of Imagisme is that it does not use images as ornaments."[5] But, of course, the movement had done just that, degenerating into the otiose and charmingly conversational poses of "Amygism." Pound's demand, as Oppen saw it, was ethical.

THE GESTURE

The question is: how does one hold an apple
Who likes apples

And how does one handle
Filth? The question is

How does one hold something
In the mind which he intends

To grasp and how does the salesman
Hold a bauble he intends

> To sell? The question is
> When will there not be a hundred
>
> Poets who mistake that gesture
> For a style.
>> (from "Five Poems About Poetry," *Collected Poems*)[6]

Ethical how? William Carlos Williams had said that "imagism failed because it lost structural necessity."[7] Hulme's "moon like a ruddy-faced farmer," the "wistful stars" with children's faces of the same poem, were not, Zukofsky might have commented, "thinking with things as they exist" but wishing sentimentalities into things which they did not have.

The Objectivists embody a direction implicit in Williams' comments on Pound that "the principal move in imaginative writing today [is] that away from the word as a symbol toward the word as reality."[8] Words are real, in the Objectivist formulation, because they instate an existence beyond the words. They are an expression of a "faith"—as Oppen speaks of it in describing his own poetics—"that the nouns do refer to something; that it's there, that it's true, the whole implication of these nouns; that appearances represent reality, whether or not they misrepresent it."[9] Zukofsky, suggesting much the same thing, maintains in "An Objective," that seminal working paper of Objectivist thought, that "the economy of presentation in writing is a reassertion of faith that the combined letters—the words—are absolute symbols for objects, states, acts, interrelations, thoughts about them. If not, why use words—new or old?"[10]

Pound had of course meant something similar by his Imagist "dos and don'ts" remark that "the natural object is always the adequate symbol."[11] But beyond this notion of word and reality shared by the Objectivists and Pound, shared indeed by all the poets who come out of what Laszlo Géfin has called the "ideogrammic stream,"[12] is a deeper concern, one which marks off a significant difference between the poets of a purely Poundian lineage, Olson in particular, and the Objectivists.

Pound, in his ransackings and appropriations of history, finds, to use the Objectivist terminology of Zukofsky, elements of "objectification" already preformed in history, in the "luminous details"[13] of a poet's scholarship. The poet's "vortex" involves constructing these into an articulate, paratactical ordering, a juxtapositional relation,[14] as Géfin calls it, in which meanings never made explicit before, show forth, as it were, *between* the elements. The Poundian "pith" in this sense is an already configured, often historically-bound, piece of language which enters a poem like *The Cantos* with the rhetorical force of rule or maxim. At the same time, it is a datum, among other like data, within the constellated mass of planes and angles of the poem, to be inspired by or taught from.

Zukofsky, concerned not only with "objectification" but also with the "sincerity" of the datum, might abjure such a poetics, seeing in Pound's recuperation of, among other things, the poetry of the past, a poetics of nostalgia in that Pound's ransackings and inclusions draw their authority not from present testability but from their very pastness. The aura of pastness gives them an Arnoldian "touchstone" quality, a ticket of admittance to the "ne'er so well expressed" catalog of anthologies. For, if Objectivist "sincerity" means anything, it is not there simply to imply authentic connection with what is being said or with accurate rendition. Rather, sincerity within the Objectivist context is a bearing, a grace under pressure of alternative, consoling, imaginative schemes. What is meant to convince about Objectivist poetry is its sense of having been created within, as Zukofsky states, a "context based on the world."[15] The poem, as Zukofsky puts it a few words later, has to be "a job."[16] Thus, the division of Poundian and Objectivist poetics strikes me as hinging on this difference: that in Objectivist poetry, there is a profound sense "of one's time," that the retort from which one forges any line of verse must first pass through the furnace of personality and history. Valèry, at the turn of the century, may have said it most carefully: "Form is costly."

Oppen, in describing his "faith," also marks himself off from the Poundian scholar/historian/poet. For Oppen, words do not only consist of the lexicon of the real but are to be used also as an Objectivist "test of sincerity—that there is a moment, an actual time, when you believe something to be true, and you construct a meaning from these moments of conviction."[17] But this sense of a "moment" in which truth arises involves an attitude toward history which, again, is somewhat at odds with Pound's. In Pound, history offers up its lessons and models, provides possible dictates for behavior and for culture at large; but in Oppen, and, as I shall try to show, in the other Objectivists, no such fortuitous exempla are to be found. Rather, truth is a possible and tentative occurrence—an activity of the poet's making within the creative act of the poem. The poem does not so much show forth truth as it shows forth the "conviction" (and hence the sincerity) of the moment, a moment which is time-bound and provisional, historical only in the sense that behind it lies the poet's knowledge of history and his world. One does not live *by* such poetry as the Objectivists write, but with and through it. Nor does one enter history or historical interpretation, as one often does with Pound; instead, one enters a temporality which bears history's burdens. This temporality, manifest in various and different ways depending on the particular poet one is examining, is advanced, not as truth or moral precept, but as something which, according to Oppen, "cannot not be understood."[18] In other words, if Pound's poetry is, in my reading of it here, declamatory, a dispensation of culture and ethics, then the Objectivist poem, by contrast, is communicative, intersubjective, in that it wishes to entangle its reader in its momentary convictions. Behind Zukofsky's sense of "objectification" is not so much a doctrine of impersonality but one of sufficient thing-ness (to use a Heideggerian expression), of human used-ness, which means to convince one of the actuality of the poem in hand. Rachel Blau DuPlessis, in writing of the distinction between Pound and Oppen, puts it clearly when she says of the latter's work that it is a "texture of affiliation." [19] Such a poetry attains, if not to scientific truthfulness, to a quality of being "true" to one's time.

An aside: pragmatist Charles Saunders Peirce once remarked that the definition of truth is that which we are prepared to act on. Our recent American history is an exemplum of the consequences of investing things (Mom, the presidency, pax Americana) with sentimentalities to the point of their being taken for truths. To the extent that poets are unacknowledged legislators of social and political life, their ethical role might be likened to keeping things honest, with regard to language at least. Among our poetries, the Objectivists stand out as a salutary force, as a flying poetic truth squad. Of interest to the social historian would be the resonances of Oppen's reworking of Populism, Reznikoff's urban poetry, Rakosi's *Americana* series and the cleansing force of Zukofsky's poetic theories.

Zukofsky once wrote:

> To me *Bottom: On Shakespeare* is [among other things]: A long poem built on a theme for the variety of its recurrences. The theme is simply that Shakespeare's text throughout favors the clear physical eye against the erring brain, and that this theme has historical implications. [20]

Bottom is the summit of Objectivist thought: complex, various and meant to "take exception to all philosophies from Shakespeare's point of view," [21] it is the neglected masterwork of our era.

The blurb-writing editors of *The Norton Anthology of Modern Poetry* (which conspicuously omits all of the Objectivists but Zukofsky), taking their cue from the statement above, and not, it would seem, from the work itself, object that Zukofsky's reading of Shakespeare is only partial. One might better say that his reading is American, concerned less with the collapsing fates of those on the Great Chain of Being than with a certain democratization of Shakespeare's eye, with the way human character is fully treated in the plays. Of each character,

Zukofsky formulates: "Their *means* equal their *extremes*" when "*love is to reason as the eyes are to mind.*"[22]

Zukofsky's theme is long and elaborate, entailing much of Western culture's literary and philosophical signposts from Aristotle to Wittgenstein. Poetic rather than discursive in nature, its meaning cannot be summarized or paraphrased but must be experienced. *Bottom* is excursus, hint, and suggestion, the basis of its argument being that Shakespeare's democracy of characters, i.e., that all are given complete and human, is the result of the totality of Shakespeare's vision. And that totality—its openness to every variety and mode of experience—transcends any philosophical or conceptual base. It is not the purpose of this study to examine *Bottom*; however, its notion of democratization is implied in its use of quotations, as for instance in the following from Whitman:

> The greatest poet forms the consistence of what is to be from what has been and is . . . The greatest poet has less a marked style, is more *the channel of thoughts and things without increase or diminuation*, and is the free channel of himself . . . I will have nothing hang in the way, not the richest curtains. (1855 Preface to *Leaves of Grass*)[23]

What *Bottom: On Shakespeare* argues, as it "reads" Shakespeare's canon, is a visual-materialist methodology of human relations, history and knowledge. As this study will attempt to show, the Objectivist terminology of sincerity and objectification is but another modality for the democratization of Zukofsky's clear physical eye.

Whitman's Paumanouk argument, his statements above, versed, might read as follows:

> What can be compared to
> the living eye?
> Its East
> is flowering
> honeysuckle

> and its North
> dogwood bushes.
>
> . . . .
>
> Who is like man
>   sitting in the cell
> of referents . . .
>
> It is the great eye
>   source of security.
> Praised be thou,
>   as the Jews say,
> who have engraved clarity
> and delivered us to the mind
>   where you must
> reign severe as quiddity of bone
>   forever and ever
> without bias or mercy
> without attrition or mystery.
>   (Carl Rakosi, "Associations with A
>   View from the House")[24]

Here, it would seem, we have entered a phenomenological
precinct where "without bias or mercy" not only tempers praise
but suggests, to be philosophical, the eye's truth-value. After
all, it is quite possible that one does not like what one sees.
Nevertheless, the world is there to be seen, to be endured against
a comforting set of illusions, sentimentalities and the like.
Whatever differences the Objectivists have (and there are many),
they all seem bent on discovering what Merleau-Ponty has called
"the decisive moment of perception: the upsurge of a true and
accurate world."[25] As Oppen puts it:

> River of our substance
> Flowing
> With the rest. River of our substance
> Of the earth's curve, river of the substance

> Of the sunrise, river of silt, of erosion, flowing
> To no imaginable sea. But the mind rises
>
> Into happiness, rising
>
> Into what is there. I know of no other happiness
> Nor have I ever witnessed it . . .
> (from "A Narrative," *Collected Poems*)[26]

This is surely a happiness as democratic as Shakespeare's eye or Whitman's soul. And surely it rests without bias or mercy, is akin, as Oppen says elsewhere, to the philosopher's sense of wonder.

> It is impossible the world be either good or bad
> If its colors are beautiful or if they are not beautiful
> If parts of it taste good or if no parts of it taste good
> It is as remarkable in one case as the other
> (from "Seascape: Needle's Eye," *Collected Poems*)[27]

Let us revert to some comparative literature. From the Objectivist point of view, the world is endured, literally lived with in time, as opposed to used. The poem is "concerned with a fact which it did not create."[28] For the Objectivists, echoing Whitman, the world is fact, and the poet is its agency.

With a poet like Robert Lowell, on the other hand, who seems to represent the summit of another tradition, the world is taken as an agency and the poet is the fact. For example, Lowell's vision (again in the little v sense) is more likely to be what a psychologist would call projection.

> My whole eye was sunset red
> the old cut cornea throbbed,
> I saw things darkly,
> as through an unwashed goldfish globe

The shift from the medical to the metaphysical is immediate:

> Outside the summer rain
> a simmer of rot and renewal

. . . .

> Nothing can dislodge
> the triangular blot
> No ease from the eye
> of the sharp-shinned hawk in the birdbook there

And on to a conclusive conclusion:

> Nothing. No oil
> for the eye, nothing to pour
> on those waters or flames.
> I am tired. Everyone's tired of my turmoil.[29]

A study of Lowell's imagery, particularly of his depiction of the natural world, will reveal such usage again and again. What we get in Lowell often enough is a state of mind, yet one presented without the givens which produced that mind's pain. It is a fallen world into which its author—a fallen poet—presumes, we, too, are willing to fall. Such poetry is not without an element of guilt.

What is quite astonishing about the Objectivists, however, is that the entire canon is almost totally free of the guilty conscience of so much modern poetry. Against this guilt stands the Objectivist weapon of the clear physical eye, yet an eye that is by no means naive. It is an eye "against the erring brain," the brain of concepts, projections, personal fears and desires, an eye desirous of seeing what is and thus taking the risk of going beyond the old hubris, beyond one's attachment to ego, pain and self-indulgence. In his book *A Homemade World*, Hugh Kenner says the motto of the Objectivists might well be "No myths."[30]

Let me interpose a crude retrospect: one does not have to be a missionary of the secular to understand what Baudelaire meant by saying that "civilization does not consist in steam or electricity, but in the diminution of the traces of original sin."[31] Had Baudelaire been reading Whitman, he would have understood in that one figure how far along America was, in its own stupendous way, toward working out formulae for such diminutions. For most of Europe, there were, and would be for a time, the two worlds of the sacred and the profane. Yeats is perhaps the last great energizer of that condition: "And gather me / into the artifice of eternity. / Once out of nature I shall never take / my bodily form from any natural thing" (*Sailing to Byzantium*)[32] Whitman, some sixty years before, had already begun America's long sail away from Byzantium. He had reconciled the two worlds in the imagination: "I am the poet of the soul and I am the poet of the body / the pleasures of heaven . . . the pain of hell are with me."[33]

Much contemporary poetry, its governing body at least, seems to have taken to half of Whitman's declamation: the divinity of self. (It has, in addition, insisted *ad nauseum* that "the pains of hell are with me.") In this contemporary poetry, as with Lowell, the world is metaphorized, the objective correlative is found, which gives the reader knowledge of the poet's pain. It may be said that confessionalism and surrealism, the most widely found modes in contemporary poetry, are often involved in a manipulation of the visible contents of the world. Objectivist work, by contrast, appears as a rendition, an approximation to, rather than a manipulation of, those contents.

Looking back, like a stern child on a wayward parent, the Objectivist would seek to impose the language and rigor of the visible world as "structural necessity" on Imagist techniques. Let us return again to Zukofsky's remark that "the economy of presentation in writing is a reassertion of faith that . . . the words—are absolute symbols for objects, states, acts, interrelations, thoughts about them."[34]

If one's vehicle of realization is poetry—and here I am pushing Zukofsky's idea to its extreme—if one's poetry is not merely a swapping of one abstraction for another, if one is trying to look past one's settled conceptions of the world, then one is involved in an extremely crucial situation: one is involved in seeing, seeing with the clear physical eye. And the intensity of that situation arises when, as Oppen puts it, "the difference between just the neurosensitivity of the eye and the act of seeing is one over which we have no control."[35] The eye opens to knowledge, take it or leave it, but in the poem, the world starts up again. The moment of perception is decisive, not because it is unconditioned, but because it is conditioned substantially against the old mythologies—the eye of the poet cannot be naive if we are to have songs of experience, not innocence.

> Because the known and the unknown
> Touch
>
> One witnesses—
> It is ennobling
> If one thinks so.
>
> If to know is noble
>
> It is ennobling
> (George Oppen, "Of Being Numerous")[36]

Again, Kenner says it finely: "No myths might be the Objectivist motto."[37]

For much of contemporary poetry, the poet is the central fact of the poem, the world an arena for emotions. The effect is, through metaphor, image and symbol, not unlike projection. Yet there are other epiphanies. The Objectivist version of the image is something which "is a factor of realistic art, of realist art in that the poem is concerned with a fact which it did not create" (Oppen), which "thinks with things as they exist" (Zukofsky). Of the modern movements in poetry, the Objectivist movement falls least under Auden's term of "alternate worlds." Against the modern hubris, the Objectivist poem strangely consoles, returns us to our home.

> It is true the great mineral silence
> Vibrates, hums, a process
> Completing itself

In which the windshield wipers
Of the cars are visible.

The power of the mind, the
Power and weight
of the mind which
Is not enough, it is nothing
And does nothing

Against the natural world,
Behemoth, white whale, beast
They will say and less than beast,
The fatal rock

Which is the world—

O if the streets
Seem bright enough,
Fold within fold
Of residence . . .

Or see thru water
Clearly the pebbles
Of the beach
Thru the water, flowing
From the ripple, clear
As ever they have been
                    (George Oppen, "Of Being Numerous")[38]

As to witnessing, that, too, reaches a kind of upper limit in Objectivist writing. Reznikoff, the poet-witness *par excellence*, demonstrates, particularly in *Testimony* and *Holocaust* (works selected and edited from courtroom documents and war records), an almost pure receptivity to his material. The works are without the usual nuances of style and manner, yet, litanies of horrors that they are, they are far from being the case of an author's abscondence. Instead, the authorial neutrality becomes a way of implicating the broadest range of social, political and philosophical responses in a confrontation with material about which it would seem, the less said, the better. These are things, to use Rakosi's phrase, that are witnessed "without bias or mercy."

The American "something" which Fauchereau sees in the Objectivists might be tracked, speculated on as follows: Whitman had begun the modern secularization of the self ("Objects gross and the unseen soul are one"); this was an attempt at reconciling our mythologies—religious, social and democratic—with our actual state of affairs, an attempted conversion of our myths into lessons. The Objectivists, in their preference for the clear physical eye over "the erring brain," are the direct inheritors of that aspect of Whitman. Never mind that the world, least of all the New World, is not as we might wish it. The gift of the Objectivists is the gift of "what has been and is," "the consistence of what is to be," a truly prophetic art.

2 Louis Zukofsky's Objectivist Poetics: Reflections and Extensions

Some time ago I wrote in my notebook: "Zukofsky's poetics—timely, timeless." They are timely and timeless in that one can always return to such statements as those in *Prepositions* or in the poems of *A* and *All* and recover the sense of being a poet, recover the sense or nonsense of a modality of craft. Zukofsky's writings on poetry, like his poems, were, in the most profound sense, objective—not so much impersonal, as given without partisanship. They were not in the service of advancing some "school" but of returning the poet who might read them to the very beginnings and impulses of poetic art. One of the key passages, often quoted and considered by many to be a kind of ur-statement of Objectivist poetics, is the following:

> In sincerity shapes appear concomitants of word combinations, precursors of (if there is continuance) completed sound or structure, melody or form. Writing occurs which is the detail, not mirage, of seeing, of thinking with things as they exist, and of directing them along a line of melody. Shapes suggest themselves, and the mind senses and receives awareness. Parallels sought for in the other arts call up the perfect line of

occasional drawing, the clear beginnings of sculpture not pro-
ceeded with.

Presented with sincerity, the mind even tends to supply, in
further suggestion, which does not attain rested totality, the to-
tality not always found in sincerity and necessary only for per-
fect rest, complete appreciation. This rested totality may be called
objectification—the apprehension satisfied completely as to the
appearance of the art form as an object. That is: distinct from
print which records action and existence and incites the mind
to further suggestions, there exists, though it may not be har-
bored as solidity in the crook of an elbow, writing (audibility in
two-dimensional print) which is an object or affects the mind as
such. The codifications of the rhetoric books may have some-
thing to do with an explanation of this attainment, but its char-
acter may be simply described as the arrangement, into one
apprehended unit, of minor units of sincerity—in other words,
the resolving of words and their ideation into structure.[1]

This passage—the central excerpt from Zukofsky's "An Ob-
jective," a critical "statement" prompted in part by Harriet
Monroe's desires to subsume Zukofsky's selections for *Poetry*
under the aegis of a "movement"—contains the key terms of
Zukofsky's poetics, those which mark off Objectivist poetics from
both traditional formulae and from the modernist poetics of
Pound and even Williams. The most important of these, the
three notions of sincerity, objectification and rested totality, were
to become the parameters by which Objectivist poetry was to
be defined.

Yet these terms, as Zukofsky uses and reuses them, imply
less a stance or method from which poems are to be con-
structed than a set of boundary markers in the proximity of
which poetic activity may be said to take place and, in a sense,
to be measured. The aim of such measuring is not to establish
criteria or standards (though examples of "standards" are both
given and implied) but to provide guidelines and further sub-
tilizing means to be used by the poet in considering the act of
writing. Around these terms, the poet—certainly each of the

Objectivist poets discussed in this study—has interwoven his or her own field of possibility. In the notes which follow, I have been less concerned with tightly defining Zukofsky's terms than with evoking the feeling tone which the terminology suggests, with presenting the "field," so to speak, posited by the vocabulary.

Zukofsky's poetics continue to attract because they embrace a remarkable rigor within a frame of generosity and openness. The rigor, by being related through the term "objectification" to our notions about the world or about nature, unfolds towards a factual or experiential openness, whereas generosity, by being under the sign of such terms as "truth" and "sincerity," becomes a formal rigor. Such an embrace seems to make of Zukofsky's poetics more a code of honor, a way of being in the world, and only in the most general sense a matter of stylistics. With respect to style, what Zukofsky's poetics communicate has more the quality of a pressure than that of enforceable axioms or injunctions. Thus, Zukofsky's "In sincerity shapes appear concomitants of word combinations"[2] is both a beginning and an end of a poetics, one which seeks to be of the world and yet be a world. Such a poetics takes the world as its necessary condition, a condition in the most basic sense that words stand for it, that words, as Zukofsky says elsewhere, are "metaphor enough." Thus, the force of the poetics is toward a perfect parity in context between what is and what is said, towards the necessary and away from the merely arbitrary means by which poems get written.

At the same time, Zukofsky's poetics recognize that the "arbitrary" is, at the least, a salient aspect of the world. Thus, in his poem "Mantis," a sestina with its own "interpretation" about encountering a praying mantis in the subway, Zukofsky writes: "The mantis itself only an incident, *compelling any writing*."[3] Yet, in engaging this incident, any incident, the poet does not so much embrace absurdity and chaos as enter into a partnership with them, for, as Zukofsky goes on to suggest, the incidental, "the mantis *can start* / History, etc . . . Enough worth if the emotions can equate it."[4] That equation, the poem, so Zukofsky's poetics assert, can rescue the human character of the world from the world, from its indifference, from simple otherness; hence, "objectivity" or "Objectivist" has a special meaning in Zukofsky's work.

His terminology, Zukofsky's poetics argue, is not concerned with the reified objectification of knowledge into a science, which is fulfilled, so we are told, with or without us, but with an objectification of human instance, of witnessing (active) or being witnessed, as in that peculiar rendition or transformation wherein

> . . . whatever has been read,
>   whatever is heard,
>   whatever is seen
> Perhaps goes back cropping up again with
> Inevitable recurrence again in the blood
> Where the spaces of verse are not visual
> But a movement, . . .
>   (from "Mantis," *All*)[5]

And it might be remarked that the "Perhaps" above is singularly important because it leaves the occasion open for yet more concrete or palpable definitions; Zukofsky is as wary as any writer of "locking up" a perception—aware, as well, of the slippery nature of form. Rather, a poem is or ought to be a precise rendition of temporality, a fleeting judgment of an occasion, so that the poet may feel that, at least, he speaks for or towards an ever unlimited truth rather than the Truth, achieving this by making his little "t" truth as full and inclusive as its moment will allow.

Zukofsky's poetics remind us, against much contemporary critical fashion, how the human and the worldly touch, how meaning is not to be evaded. Speaking of hearing Homer in the Greek, he insists that such audition is

> ... to 'tune in' to the human tradition, to its voice *which has developed among the sounds of natural things*, and thus escapes the confines of a time and place, . . . (my italics)[6]

This is to say that according to Zukofsky, what we call tradition is simply meanings offered and meanings surpassed by meanings offered, etc., a wheel which even surrealism could not get off because there is finally no alternative to the structuring of experience by humans. And these meanings are more or less inclusive than those which they surpass because they are temporal—not pejoratively—and because they embrace both the sense and nonsense of their time and are altered by both our "progress" and our forgetfulness.

Such a sense of tradition, as both a historical and a temporal grounding, makes Zukofsky's poetics useful: they form a base line from which to see the writing of our time, making us aware, for instance, of what may be lost through our own cleverness and metaphorical capaciousness, as when he says in *"Mantis"*:

> No human being wishes to become
> An insect for the sake of a symbol[7]

Zukofsky's lines here may be likened to a rejoinder to the political as well as the poetical thinkers who exclude (or include) the persuasive symbology of contemporary poetry on rhetorical rather than reasonable grounds.

If it strikes one that Zukofsky's poetics are to the poetry of our time as Ockham's razor was to the sciences, that there is indeed a certain parsimony to both the poetics and the poetry which arises from it, it would be well to recall under what conditions Zukofsky's work manifests itself, how it is (in the face of, as Williams so aptly put it, "what passes for the new") a profoundly conservative effort. Furthermore, one has to consider that its value for the poet lies precisely in its conservatory nature, a nature which is yet open to the possibility of any linguistic usage as long as that usage grounds us in the world, as long as it appears to be necessary and neither dilution nor decor.

"Desire is no excess," Zukofsky says in *All*. Desire as praise, as love or understanding is not a redundance but a further relation, enlargement as opposed to analogy. So that parsimony obtains even within desirability: the relationship is exhausted in saying all one can say, but not more. And the world enters here to save the poet from incomprehensibility or infiniteness because his words exhaust relation by returning to the world the way they (the words) must have once seemed to arise from it (see the quotation above regarding Homer). I take it that this "saying all there is" is Zukofsky's rested totality.

And yet, neither the world nor the perceiving mind is at rest in the sense of unaltering fixity; the poem is at rest—the poem's judgment of temporality—which allows the remainder of the world release, as when the act of vision focuses on a house or a tree, and all else is in abeyance, is only negatively implied.

"Nature as creator"—the poet synthesizing, structuring, and allowing himself to be structured. The poem (and the poet writing it) encounters and makes use of what is seen and known by remaining subject to experiential and intellectual pressures.*

> A poem, A poem as object—And yet certainly it arose in the veins and capillaries, if only in the intelligence—Experienced—(every word can't be over-defined) experienced as object—Perfect rest—Or nature as creator, existing perfect, experience perfecting activity of existence, making it—theologically, perhaps like the Ineffable—[8]

"Ineffable" not because it is unsaid or indecipherable, but because, said so well, it engenders an awe of completeness.

*One distinguishes, however, as Heidegger suggested, "between an object of scholarship and a matter of thought."

3 The Poetry of Louis Zukofsky: To Draw Speech

Take care, song, that what stars' imprint you mirror
Grazes their tears; draw speech from their nature or
Love in you—faced to your outer stars—purer
Gold than tongues make without feeling
                                    —*Louis Zukofsky, A–11* [1]

Reluctant "Objectivist" labeler, theorizer, poet, as in his great exploration of Shakespeare, *Bottom: On Shakespeare,* meant, among other things, to put an end to philosophy, Zukofsky stands outside and beyond any categorization, including that of "Objectivist." Zukofsky's work is not only multifaceted but each facet also entails and bears on every other facet. The resulting complexity, resistant to any straightline interpretation, imparts a classical status to Zukofsky's work. Indeed, the work, like the classic literary text, suggests both wholeness and a kind of useful indeterminacy, presenting different appeals and understandings to different readings. This complexity, with its endless perspectives of interest and difficulty, has been duly noted by critics of Zukofsky's poetry. Kenner, for example, in speaking of Zukofsky's major work *A*, has called it "the most hermetic poem in English, [one] which they will still be elucidating in the 22nd century."[2]

A, which Zukofsky described at times as an "epic," suggests a reinvention of that classical form; for the poem, running over eight hundred pages in length and involving some fifty years in its making, is less concerned with the actions of some hero than with the possibilities of attention. Thus, it is an epic of the mind at play, of intelligence and imagination cast into forms of possibility. Nothing distinguishes Zukofsky more from other contemporary poets—and thinkers—as this capacity of his to let the mind lead him on, to follow arcs of thought or the traceries of sound and imagery. The many contours of Zukofsky's work do not lead back into encapsulating forms or closed conceptual systems. Rather, they display the imagination reaching toward and into existence, a reaching which has an almost sacred character about it, as large in its concerns as those of religion or theology. Zukofsky's work manifests a kind of faith, not in systems of belief, but in a nearly unimaginable curiosity.

Yet Zukofsky's imagining is never perceived by the reader as something free-form; it seems, instead, in its manifold operations, in the great tonal and formal variety of the work, to be a kind of poise. In Zukofsky, we sense the whole tradition of poetry in a kind of attentive readiness.* This is not so much to see the figure of the poet in some kind of hardened "stance" but to imagine Zukofsky, as the poet and critic Harold Schimmel conjures him, playing on the resistances of poetry like a gull sinking into an air current and rising on it."[3]

Zukofsky's play with poetic resistances involves the mind's attempt not only to capture existence but to make use of and thereby "test" imagining within poetic tradition. The "test of poetry," Zukofsky writes in the preface to *A Test of Poetry*, a

---

*The sources drawn on in *Bottom On: Shakespeare*, for example, constitute a major pantheon of western civilization's thinkers and writers.

handbook for poets and readers modeled somewhat after Pound's *ABCs*, "is the range of pleasure it affords as sight, sound and intellection. This is its purpose as art." This "test" involves, as the examples in the book show, consideration of what has been accomplished in the past as a beginning for work to be done in the present. The past does not dictate poetic practice but posits, as with Zukofsky's Objectivist terminology of "sincerity" and "objectification," fields of opportunities, guidelines of past accomplishments within poetic activity that approximate spiritual instruction. This sensitivity to tradition, to poetic possibility, is profoundly conservative in Zukofsky's work, resulting in a poetry that joins the Poundian commitment to "make it new" with the primary music and song-quality of the older poetries which have come before.

Because of the immense breadth and depth of Zukofsky's work, its concentrated density, no reading can be definitive. Indeed, as Don Byrd in "The Shape of Zukofsky's Canon"[5] maintains, no one work of the many in Zukofsky's oeuvre is entirely representative of his range. What is prominent throughout, however, (and this applies to Zukofsky's prose work as well as to his poetry), is its auditory qualities, its sounded-ness in every word and phrase.

All of Zukofsky's poetry exhibits an uncanny verbal intelligence, a perfected attention to sound not found in English poetry since Wyatt and Campion. We can hear this play of syllable, pitch and tone in the earliest poems Zukofsky wrote, as in the following, "discarded" poem of his late teens:

> Stay where the casement suns unapproachably high
> See where over its aerial arch
> trees appear.
>
> Force sleeps in motionless space,
> And space, to thought, lights.

Shut the eyes,
The heart has grace.

No hurt comes here, as blind derision . . .[6]

In such a poetry we sense that every word has been heard and
overheard (as Zukofsky comments in "An Objective": "Every
word can't be over-defined"), that the long "a"s and "e"s in so
many of the words have been carefully distributed so as to give
a songlike plaint to the lines. This passage also shows Zukof-
sky's way of notating a line with punctuation, of using punc-
tuation to charge and yet clarify a line with concentrated
meanings, as in "force sleeps in motionless space, / And space,
to thought, lights." When Zukofsky's poetry became available
to readers in the 1950s, this music made his work enormously
influential among such poets as Robert Duncan, Robert Cree-
ley, Denise Levertov, and Cid Corman, and for a whole gen-
eration of younger poets who saw in Zukofsky's work a bench-
mark of sincerity and authenticity. This early musical
attentiveness continually deepened and was handled more and
more skillfully in the progress of Zukofsky's later work.

In *A*, in the more occasional poems of *All*, and in the prose
and stories, this music operates, simultaneously, on a number
of levels. There is first the notion of music as example and
analogy to poetic composition. Throughout Zukofsky's work,
there are references to the music of poetry, to musical forms,
to the fugue and canon (in particular, to Bach's comments on
music), and to the poet's need to compose in terms of the ear's
hearing. Yet this emphasis on the musical analogy of the poem
is secondary to a more far-reaching concern that deals not so
much with the creation of harmonies or pleasing qualities in
one's work as with the registration, at the most profound level,
of an authentic voice.

In Zukofsky, the music of verse is the embodiment of con-
viction, the bearer, not of what has been well said or well made,
but of the incarnated understanding of the words, or under-

standing incarnated within the mind-body of the poet as lived experience. Thus, to explore the modalities and modulations of sound in Zukofsky's work is to explore not only its musical qualities but also the temporal bearing-in of the poet's understandings and perceptions, to examine how its cadences are the traces of the poet's experience, the speech drawn out of intellectual and emotional resolvings. This examination shows the work to be less representation (of all of the Objectivists, Zukofsky is the least "visual") or epistemological certainty than a reading of how things have been "taken" by the poet; that is, the poet's truth in Zukofsky is not something which has been made so as to be forced argumentatively onto the reader or hearer; instead, the welding of sound and sense within the poem, as with a musical composition, is ultimately self-referential, to be cognized by the reader as an instance of "objectification" and valued less for its applicable "truth value" than for its feel of conviction. The conviction of the work stems from the felt weight of all its parts, from the fact that it exhibits a considered quality in all aspects. Zukofsky, in answering the question "what is good poetry?" in "A Statement For Poetry," maintains that poetry grows out of "precise information on existence" and that "rhythm, pulse, keeping time with existence is the distinction of its technique." He goes on to state that "if read properly, good poetry does not argue its attitudes or beliefs; it exists independently of the reader's preference for one kind of 'subject' or another."[7]

Scattered throughout the "epic" concerns of *A* (Zukofsky called it "the poem of a life") are the poet's insistences on the conditions under which an authentic music is to be created.

Written in mid-poem, mid-career (Zukofsky was in his middle forties at the time of its composition), the *A–12* section is, among other things, one of the fullest explorations of Zukofsky's poetics and its transformation into poetry. As signaled in its italicized opening line *"Out of deep need,"*[8] what is to follow in *A–12* has less the quality of a defense of poetry than that of a heartfelt "coming to terms" with one's own understandings, a reflection of a need to profess one's making of poems as integral to the meaning of being human, of existing with a world, a culture and a family. *A–12* is to bear the burden implied in the lines from *A–11* quoted at the beginning of this discussion: to "draw speech from their nature or / love in you." This drawing of speech (drawing in the double sense of extracting as well as inscribing) and the poem itself will have necessary conviction only as they satisfiy the Objectivist criteria of sincerity and objectification. These criteria are, for Zukofsky, exemplified in musical form, in particular in the musical forms of the baroque and classical periods with their muted programmatic intention. In the works of Bach or Handel, for instance, the "meaning" is not in the creation or coloration of some occurrence external to the music but is, in the most profound sense, in the music itself, in the interrelations of notes, themes, tonal effects, etc. The sense of totality or completeness of such music is in its absence of a residue, in its simultaneity of means and ends.

Zukofsky does not equate poetry with music, but he sees in the musical model the poet's aspiration. As he says in "An Objective": "The order of all poetry is to approach a state of music wherein the ideas present themselves sensuously and intelligently and are of no predatory intent."[9] In "A Statement For Poetry," he describes poetry as "an order of words that . . . approaches in varying degrees the wordless art of music . . ."[10] Thus, in *A–12*, Zukofsky states:

I'll tell you.
About my poetics—

∫ music

speech

An integral
lower limit speech
upper limit music.[11]

If we are to read Zukofsky's poetry properly, we must regard the poem as neither music nor speech but as something which moves, or is created within, the integral limits given above. Poetry, in Zukofsky's formulations, can never be music since it consists of words, which carry not only sounds but definitional and associative meanings; nor can poetry ever be speech alone, since the meaning of words is not only lexical or contextual but also individual, subject to how they are sounded in the poet's world, history and experience. In Zukofsky's poetics, the poet has to accommodate or deal with the tension between these two aspects of language. It is in their objectified resolution that poetry arises. Such a resolution involves the transcending and linking notion of "word," not only as both sound (or music) and meaning but also as referent: words, as Zukofsky puts it, as "absolute symbols for objects, states, acts, interrelations, thoughts about them."[12]

If, for the Objectivists, words are real, that realness results in this "absolute" symbolism, which gives words both substantive and gestural weight, for gesture, interactivity and penetration between subjects are all implied in Zukofsky's use of the word "symbol." The poet, Zukofsky seems to suggest, creates things to be read, creates "that order which can speak to all men." The symbol as here mediated by Zukofsky is not so much the usual self-contained literary entity to be appreciated and decoded, but a construct of words created by the poet so that the world can be read. The entangled meaning and music of poetry is, above all else, communicative, or, in Zukofsky's words, "specific information about existence."

This specificity has about it a moral burden: the Objectivist poet, meaning to inform, to convey or translate to the reader the existence which he knows through the media of objectification and sincerity, must resist not only the aleatory, freewheeling associativeness of words but also the usual decorative conceit of the symbol or image. Zukofsky rejects the poetry of the strained metaphor on moral grounds because "it carries the mind by a diffuse everywhere and leaves it nowhere."[13]

This sense of poetry, while seeming to reject the easy symbol making and surrealism of much contemporary American poetry, is not, in Zukofsky, reductive; nor is it aimed particularly at some instrumental theory of poetry. Rather, as with Aristotle (one of the touchstones of Zukofsky's poetics and critical writings), the taking up of language is seen as an intersubjective act, hemmed round with convictions and suspicions that there are worlds and readers out there. One's language in all its manifestations (poetry, prose, etc.) has affect, and its use, therefore, involves ethical considerations.

This flavor of ethical concern permeates every aspect of Zukofsky's work. Objectification and sincerity are not simply tools to write good poems with; they represent forms of value, aspirations, and mediations of experience between poet and reader. As Zukofsky says in "An Objective": "We shall never know how to dispose of our sensations before we begin to read poetry, or how to raise them to honesty or intelligence."[14] Zukofsky's thought here continually bears in on the responsibility of communication, on creating effects. In keeping with Aristotle's claim that "poetry is both more philosophic and graver than history," Zukofsky maintains that the objectified yet sincere creation in language which one calls poetry is, or should be, the most complete communication obtainable. This poetry, as incarnated meaning, as meaning which has been worked, so to speak, within the mind-body of the poet, is superior to the generalizations of science and to the conventionalized discourse of prose.

What marks poetry off from prose in this sense is its creative or anti-entropic nature, for if conventional prose is an end in explanation, poetry, by its objective character and by its appeal to the emotions as well as the intellect—that is, presuming some dichotomy exists between the two—presents a complete and solidified entity to interact with. As Zukofsky says of poetry in *A–12*:

> From my body to other bodies
> Angels and bastards interchangeably
> Who had better sing and tell stories
> Before all will be abstracted.[15]

In other words, the impulse behind Objectivist poetics, as formulated by Zukofsky, lies not in presenting a better version or understanding of reality but in creating an art which aspires to complete transmissibility.

We had better sing, Zukofsky maintains, even imperfectly, or all understanding is but dead literalism. Voiced into song, the graver information of poetry lifts meanings and their associated emotions off the page and reinstalls them in the subjects of all thought: science, philosophy and poetry, human beings. Whatever this information may lose in rhetorical force by being "poeticized" so to speak, and hence no longer scientifically or rationally "objective," it regains by a voiced-as-human quality, a quality which imparts both creativity and credibility to the statement. Here we are dealing with the subtlest aspect of Zukofsky's poetry: a thought is creative not only by the newness of the information which it contains but also by the fact that it is the product of another mind, having a "his thought, not my thought" quality. Zukofsky seems to parse Spinoza for this idea in *A−12*.

> The idea
> Is not
> In the mind
> That can cut off
> Our bodies.
> To perceive a winged horse
> Affirms wings on a horse,
> They stay
> Unless another idea
> With the body as object
> Removes wings from a horse
> From the reason[16]

At the same time, this creative aspect of poetry's "information" is in tandem with a new credibility, for the thought which poetry embodies has been deinstitutionalized, removed from the oppressive categories of science and philosophy. Far from being a devaluation, the incarnated sounding of the thought (poetry) abolishes the dichotomies imposed by the separation of the individual from the knowledge of which he is the instrument. Here we can see that Zukofsky's definition of poetry as a "rested totality" is an act of reaching, a "desire for an inclusive object," as he says in "An Objective," which signals and even at times abolishes the disposition of rhetorical forces between humans and their institutions. In this lies poetry's ethical creativity.

The notion of complete transmissibility, of a poetry which is "contended" (another of Zukofsky's terms for the Objectivist goal of a rested totality), will involve, since existence is variable or fluctual, "a specialized sense for every unfolding."[17] Such a notion mediates against a formal regularity in poetry, for in concord with contemporary observations of science, psychology, and ethics, Zukofsky insists in his poem "Mantis" that "the age will not bear too regular a form." Every unfolding must find its own formal means; the poet, tuned to the immense variety of his or her experience, to the many forms in which such experience might be cast, can find in no one method the means to objectify, in poetry, his or her life. The multiplicity of shapes and perspectives in *A* and its vast number of formal devices are not the signature of an uncertain poetics but a response and demonstration to life's variousness. Zukofsky's work is a warrant, not for mastery over existence, but for nimble-minded attentiveness to its occasions. As though referring to his own work's formal ungainliness, he says in *A–12*: "Have your odyssey / How many voiced it be."[18]

The actual problems of reading posed by Zukofsky's work are analogous to the critical problem of evaluating them: how to take or account for a multiplicity of stylistic devices and intentions and not view them as some loose dispersal of Zukofsky's talent and genius. If two of the key elements by which the work should be considered are the musical analogy and the intention of complete transmission, yet another element is Zukofsky's sense of measure. Appearing and reappearing throughout *A–12*, almost as litany or reminder, is the line "Measure, tacit is." [19] This measure, Zukofsky's work argues, is the element through which awareness is ordered. The poet, encountering acts, people, events, thoughts, seeks first to clarify his understanding of what he or she has encountered. The "tacit" employment of a measure is a resistance to preformed or preconceptualized notions of world or poem. It is an almost physical refusal to employ the quick take, to fix or lock up thought or poem within existing literary, cultural, or philosophical systems. The aims of measure are not mastery of experience but clarification and hence communication. The poet, Zukofsky tells us, is concerned with the "proper conduct" of making his poem, "a concern to avoid clutter no matter how many details outside and inside the head are ordered." But "this does not presume that the style will be the man, but rather that the order of his syllables will define his awareness of order." [20]

Order, then, is not an imposition but a discovery, an interactive occasion between poet and world. The capacity to give body, to produce order, is contingent on a combination of the poet's skillful use and understanding of the modalities of the past and in his sensitive attunement to the dictates of the material under hand.

But this combination, according to Zukofsky, is still not sufficient. For to measure, to order, involves taking up the intersubjective nature of language and focusing on, as it were, the art of poetry as a communicative act. This requires, as Zukofsky remarks of Shakespeare in *On Bottom: Shakespeare*, an "inexpressible trust of expression." [21] Indeed, the "tacit"-ness of Zukofsky's measuring is no mere desire to avoid arbitrary or false orderings at the expense of reality but involves a commitment to showing forth reality beyond or even at the expense of artfulness or form.

Such a sense of measure, an opening and encouragement towards the totality of existence, is the means to the poet's "proper conduct." And yet Zukofsky wants us to understand that this openness is in no way a passive or quietistic relating to the world. To perceive openly is to intend to mean fully, to be in relation with the world and, if one is a poet, with the reader. Perception and intention to mean come, as it were, together, simultaneously, as what we call a communicative act. Or, as the philosopher Merleau-Ponty has put it: "Speech and understanding are moments in the unified system of self-other."[22] Such a "moment" of measuring (the poem) is not an attempt to reach others but is the very form of our interconnectedness—in Zukofsky's words, the reflection of how we "weather division" and by that discover "the kinship of what is in what is not."[23]

For Zukofsky, this amounts to both praise and instruction, an occasion to enact and realize the poem as a place where one can "sing *in them I flourish.*"[24] For the weathering of division—in this case between reader and poem—depends upon both the art and the cumulative trusts, the ethical dimensions, at once personal and public, upon which Zukofsky has built the poem. Whatever one may make of *A*'s hermetic quality, it is not an instance of "art for art's sake." The poem might better be defined as "human for human's sake," for it is at one with Spinoza's moving denial of nihilism (in *The Ethics*), which Zukofsky so carefully delineates in *A–12*:

> I grant no one is deceived
> In so far as he perceives.
>
> The imaginations of the mind
>   in themselves
> Involve no error.
>
> But I deny that a man

> affirms nothing
> In so far as he perceives—[25]

Imagining, as given by Spinoza and Zukofsky, is not only warranted in that it enables one to speculate creatively on existence but also because, in imaginative activity, one enters a world of others.

A and the other works of Zukofsky's canon are finally demonstrations of the totality of Zukofsky's openness and inclusiveness. While only the themes of its poetics have been touched on here, it should be noted that in its great length the world of Zukofsky's family, friends, and readings, as well as history itself, both ancient and contemporary, is examined. Zukofsky treats these materials with the compassion and understanding implicit in the sage's advice quoted in *A–12*:

> Reject no one
> and
> Debase nothing.
> This is all-around intellect.[26]

Such loving intellect fulfills the timeless mandates of poetry, drawing as it does on both hymn and epiphany to measure (to "determine" as below) and, by such measure, to become language.

> Waltzing it an era
> Dusty unseen harps
> So rich in determined loss
> The loss flames and reacts
> Radiates in words.[27]

In *A*, all of existence seems wreathed in the radiative possibilities of words, and, within this radiance, Zukofsky's intentions in writing seem clear: "The best way to find out about poetry is to read poems. That way the reader becomes something of a poet himself: not because he 'contributes' to the poetry, but because he finds himself subject to its energy."[28]

Such energy, like Zukofsky's note on Mozart's "science," is both sign and service of the interrelative possibilities of the poem, for the poem has made the reader "something of a poet himself," and its inclusiveness is our inclusiveness "so that timbre understands timbre."[29]

4 Carl Rakosi: Profoundly in Between

*A passage from Maritain follows me around: to him poetry meant
'that intercommunication between the inner being of things and
the inner being of the human self which is a form of divination.'*
—*Carl Rakosi*, Ex Cranium, Night[1]

Within the larger framework of Objectivist possibilities, Carl
Rakosi's work seems to explore the ground between intercom-
munication and divination, to, indeed, propose a poetics that,
like a divining rod, sets itself between the human who wishes,
who loves, and who fears and the object of his passions. For
Rakosi's poetry shows forth the desire to possess, even as it
reminds poet and reader of deep, unbridgeable gaps between
wish and fulfillment. This poetry, then, is concerned not only
with rendering the concreteness and feel of an actual world
but also with accurately depicting the life of the emotions as
they swarm between object and person; it is an attempt to ar-
ticulate a kind of depth of field, to give substantiality to a phe-
nomenologically constructed "reality" in which the perceived
shapes of objects are dictated not only by their actuality but
also by the mind that longs after them.

Rakosi's poetry exhibits an almost Blakean affinity for the contraries and oppositions of emotional life. In contrast to the far too typical contemporary poetry of the injured ego with its due bill of insults and hurts against society and the world, Rakosi presents an exploration of the poem as the agency of personal healing and redemption, as a kind of linguistic *modus vivendi* which interweaves the traces of subject and object, of passion and passion's claim. As he puts it in one poem:

> The thing that sits self-conscious in the
> intellect and longs to be great is not the
> soul. The soul wants only a gentle planet.[2]

This thought, or certainly the spirit of this thought, is not merely one of a number of isolatable sentiments in Rakosi's work. On the contrary, Rakosi's poetry continually speaks—or brings its energy to bear, however obliquely—in opposition to the prevailing egotism of much literature. Cast against the contemporary world, Rakosi's work suggests sanity in its most transcendent form (what I would call a form of sadness and regret) by imagining the possibility of a deep relation with the world and its orderings.

> a sparrow hopping . . .
> nothing was of greater consequence . . .
> such sweetness flowing
> as through a membrane through his limbs
> the universe turned
> into a poet's enclave,
> the great society
> where simplicity is character
> and character the common tongue,
> the representative of man.
>
> In those corrupt bitter times
> the most obscure clerk
> could attain clarity
> from these poems,
> and his nature,

>   and change into a superior man
>   of exquisite modesty
>   by simply looking at a heron crossing a stream.
>   (from "The China Policy," *Ex Cranium, Night*)[3]

Rakosi's subject is the curious equation we make between
life and emotions, curious because in Rakosi we sense a poet
unconvinced of the equation's aptness. A close reading of his
work shows that above all it embodies a deep resistance to the
idea of mind (as postulated in much modern poetry) as some-
thing which desires to be possessed, to be victimized and
pounced upon by the wave of its own self-centered feelings.
Such a poetry as Rakosi's is obviously at odds with many of the
hidden guilts and resentments of our time. Indeed, his work
seems, by its very nature, to be an indirect exposé of the shabby
rhetorics, the misused formal inventiveness of much contem-
porary poetry.

"The poet", Rakosi claims, "is more modest than the an-
cient philosopher: he doesn't claim that what he has thought
out is the ultimate reality."[4] As this statement implies, Rakosi's
poetics involve a taking up of the Objectivist meaning of "ob-
jectification" within the context of self-irony and distance. Such
irony is a version of Objectivist "sincerity" cast into a comic or
investigative format. As such, we could say of Rakosi's poems
that, rather than being 'emotional', they follow the path and
texture of emotion, the curve of thought and impulse, as they
mediate among images.

Reading Rakosi, one discovers that among the Objectivists
his work embraces perhaps the widest range of emotions and
feeling tones: in the poems there is awe, humor, anger, despair.
And indeed, it can be said that his work is 'about' certain things,
that subjects give rise to sentiments, to a range of responses.
But this is to miss the character of its deeper effect, an effect
that strikes one as something between contemplation and
meditation. The poems do not really attempt to capture an
essence; they seem rather to arrive out of a middle distance, a

distance at once palpable and creative. They are the linguistic equivalent of the "patina" Rakosi mentions in an early poem, "more durable" even than the subject of the poet's perceptions.[5]

Distance of this sort is less a matter of sentiment (or sentimentality) than of recognition. It has more to do with understanding the root or ground of contemporary alienation than with bemoaning it or with seeking alleviation from its effects. This understanding is intimately connected to the techniques of Rakosi's poetry, which is based, first of all, on that loss of "aura" to objects in the world as described by Walter Benjamin in his study of Baudelaire.[6] In Benjamin, as objects and their representations in words acquire an increasingly pragmatic and utilitarian character, the sense of their human use, their luster of tradition and purposefulness, which he calls "aura," is destroyed. The rich and straightforward connections to the world and its objects fall away and are replaced by alienated and mechanized relationships. Rakosi's work is, in a sense, a response to this state of affairs. As he says in an early poem in *Amulet*:

> I am he who lost
> his father's simple power
> to touch and smell
> untouched by philosophy[7]

Rakosi's poetry is concerned with recovering the aura, the "patina" described above, and aims to become a vehicle for enabling reconnections between mind and world. But such reconnections involve a willingness on the part of the poet to dwell in that area where identity is fluctual, where things out there can no longer be defined by the pragmatic, alienated constructs dictated by modern consumerized and rationalized society. In "Instructions to the Player," Rakosi likens this area, this distance between the hardened thing and the equally hardened notion of identity, to the musical interval, a space which must be entered with both courage and tact.

Cellist,
    easy on that bow.
Not too much weeping.

Remember that the soul
    is easily agitated
and has a terror of shapelessness.
It will venture out
    but only to a doe's eye.

Let the sound out
    inner *misterioso*
but from a distance
    like the forest at night.

And do not forget
    the pause between.
That is the sweetest
and has the nature of infinity.[8]

Of this "pause," one can only say that it is profoundly in
between, that the poet is attempting to give imaginative life to
the link between subject and object. The pause is sweet, infi-
nite, i.e., saturated with possibilities even as the poet has res-
cued and formulated it out of chaos. Thus, the creative dy-
namics of such a poem lie in its ability not only to restore a link
but to suggest an opening on an infinity of linkages. Such an
opening is meant to cut through the rigidified and utilitarian
constructs that characterize contemporary life.

Rakosi's importance lies not so much in this understand-
ing as in his ability to mobilize a sense of loss and distance into
a reflexive, non-aggressive poetics; the result is a poetry of
regret without resentment, a poetry of healthy—I can think
of no better word—self-knowledge and self-consciousness.

Of course, we are talking about poetry and not philoso-
phy, and the issue of an outlook into poetry, the transcription
of a private complexity into a public document, is a matter of
craft.

In order to understand what Rakosi is doing, we have to

consider briefly what the matter of poetic technique has be-
come in the present. For the most part, craft and technique,
under our tartarean modernity, have lost their old associations,
have become ends in themselves, implicitly pointing towards
attempts at mastery and control. The resulting manipulation
of language is no longer concerned with outlook, but with a
kind of inlook, with self-regard, with an attempt to create an
object which can be sold off as an extension of personality. We
see this most clearly in the inflated imagery, in the fantasticated
surreality of the contemporary poem, in which the image has
become a matter of seduction aimed at oneself. Everything
from having paid one's dues to one's cleverness is subsumed as
product. I mention this because it is necessary to see in pre-
cisely what way Rakosi departs from this contemporary ethos,
why his use of imagery, in particular, is a kind of example for
the poet writing today.

Form and imagery with Rakosi, as with the other Objec-
tivists and with most twentieth-century modernist poets, are
less the fixed elements of a technical repertoire than they are
horizons for discovery. Rakosi remarks in a prose passage in
Ex Cranium, Night:

> Men escape from realistic limitations on the wings of an art-
> ist's fortunate intuitions about his medium.
> Yet what does *form* mean? I do not even know what it means
> to ask the question. All I know is that when I ask it, I am in the
> existential world and that it can only be answered there. The
> answer may, in fact, *be* the existential world.[9]

The passage suggests, among other possibilities, the poet's de-
sire to avoid any notion of form as imposition. Yet form there
must be, for the formal properties of the poem, the very marks
which distinguish the poem from other phenomena in the world,
are the means by which it embodies conviction. Form, seen
from this viewpoint, is not the mold into which content is poured
but something captured or rescued by the desire to give ma-
teriality (or voice) to an occasion imbedded in the existential

world. Thus, form, from this perspective, is the intersection of the desire and the occasion.

In Objectivist formulations, desire is unarmed and, in a sense, has no preconceived notions of the nature of the encounter; its only givens are appearances, emotions aroused, intellectual stimulations, that is, elements in the occasion. These, we could say, are dictated by the occasion.

In terms of the above, Rakosi's poetics can be said to be ways of entering these dictates, in particular, the dictates of seeing. Yet this entering is by no means an adopting of the Imagist's "literary" image with its overtones of strained metaphorization. Nor is Rakosi employing, strictly speaking, the Williams/Pound sense of imagery with its slight flavor of encoding and reifying reality. Instead, Rakosi's poetics are techniques for reentering the dictation, for speaking, as it were, of the "existential world," which is, in the deepest sense, both given and not given; the poetics are primarily involved in the sense of recovery which I mentioned above. Look, for instance, at this key passage from the poem "Shore Line," collected in *Amulet*:

> This is the raw data.
> A mystery translates it
> Into feeling and perception;
> Then imagination;
> Finally the hard
> Inevitable quartz
> Figure of will
>   and language[10]

Here the poet finds himself in significant relation with the "raw data," the scene come upon, and the poem is less concerned with rendering that data than with following the tracings of the "mystery" by which it is transformed into the "figure of will / and language," the "inevitable quartz" (read "rested totality") of the Objectivist poem.

It is because of this tracing, this linguistic interconnecting, that Rakosi strikes one as, above all, the poet of the lived world, the phenomenal world radiating out from us, the world under the double sign of self and otherness. And it is his sense of rootedness in that world, his tact with regard to the accuracy with which one can communicate what is not entirely given, the very humor of that situation, which constitutes the dynamics of his poems.

At Rakosi's command is the entire armament of modernist poetry: irony, complexity, a mordant hilarity, and a willingness to examine the folly of the self and that of the community. Yet underlying these is the hard classical commitment to the eye in its paradoxical function of orienting us towards otherness. In Rakosi, this function is raised to the level of morality, to a kind of open intentionality.

> Matter,
>   with this look
> I wed thee
>   and become
> thy very
>   attribute.
> I shall
>   be thy faithful
> spouse,
>   true
> to thy nature
>   ("The Vow," *Ex Cranium, Night*)[11]

The language of "The Vow" is the language of the psalm, for in Rakosi, the faculty of the eye is a religious faculty, an urge toward earthly revelation.

> It is the great eye,
>   source of security.
> Praised be thou,
>   as the Jews say,
> who have engraved clarity
> and delivered us to the mind
>   where you must

> reign severe as quiddity of bone
> > forever and ever
> without bias or mercy,
> without attrition or mystery.
> ("Associations with a View from the House," *Ex Cranium, Night*)[12]

It is a revelation because the eye's seeing cannot be manipulated. For Rakosi, the eye "reigns." It is, as referred to in another poem, the "supreme governor." This relation to sight, above all other qualities in Rakosi's work, is "Objectivist" in that it marks a departure not only from the contemporary use of imagery but also from the historical Imagism of the early twentieth century. Instead of the Imagist construction, as decidedly literary activity, the eye, for Rakosi, is what public and private history must recur to: an acknowledgment of the perceived arrangement of things, the rigor of the world's visibility as the ground of imagination. As with his fellow Objectivists, Oppen and Reznikoff, the tension of the poem, with Rakosi, is the tension between an anthropomorphically language-centered world and the world of otherness—what Rakosi elsewhere calls "the soundless order."

Looked at from yet another point of view, Rakosi's craft is, in its own way, an act not only of discovery but also of permission. The clarity of line and the measured, sometimes hesitant cadences are means for admitting material into the structure of the poem. One sees this clearly in the earlier, less "existential" work, where there is a cluttering of objects, often a catalog of metonymies meant to re-create or hint at an entire structure of reality, of relations, by the most economical means, as for example, in "The City" (1925), a poem which strikes a tone somewhere between the idiomatic style of Williams and the connotative procedures of Pound.

> gilders, stampers, pen-makers, goldbeaters,

> fear of thunder
> speed
> the whore

indifference
son
  glioma
  water

Tammany, McCoy,
the bronze doors of the Guaranty Trust,
the copper spandrels.

(from *Amulet*)[13]

Rakosi's admittance of these materials is an expression of unconditional curiosity, of an active desire to be with the things of the world, the wedding of vision and mind, which, for Rakosi, is a joy almost before all others.

In Rakosi's later work, in accordance with his existential poetics, the act of perception is transformed. It becomes the exacting rendition of the physical world as both the ground of our psychology and the possibility of a simultaneity of existential modes.

Lakes being
            timeless,
yet in time.
            I have lost
my identity.
            The light
makes me
            invent nymphs . . .
and hang on
            exclamation marks . . .
and call to them
            and they call back.

Must be
            how myths arose,
the distant
            luminous ones,
motionless
            as in eternity.
("Little Observations at Yaddo," *Ex Cranium, Night*)[14]

Here, between the seen and the seer, only contingency exists, exists as thought, as possibility, that is, as language. Rakosi is the poet of this contingency; the substantive quality of his work lies not in the things it renders but in this arrested quality, the shapely contour of interacting thought and emotion, thought and object. In this sense, we could say that the possibility of possession and identification is given up for the sake of communication, or that in terms of its readers, Rakosi's work enacts a kind of rescue.

> For approaching a mystery
> to a field of force
> is the symbol.
>
> For approaching a mystery
> and for transcending,
> which is the origin of human nature
> and where all value is
> as beauty is in the eye,
> there is a ceremony.
>
> So we must get on with the poem.
> ("The Poet: VI," *Ex Cranium, Night*)[15]

There is nothing more elusive to the critical mind than this kind of work. Perhaps it is that, finally, all questions of art, in a master's hands, become subsumed under the question or quality of their humaneness and, at the same time, involve a totality or bearing which does not easily lend itself to exegesis. This totality demands of us the giving up of preconceptions and biases. Rakosi's late work, certainly, is of such a character. To be a mediator between things, and thus to be able to give up for a moment all egocentric views, all flimsy and abstract humanism, is perhaps to be most human after all. Rakosi's work is among the most compassionate bodies of poetry, compassionate because so much seems to be transformed for the express purposes of communication and seems to have been given over to directness of statement and the recognition that another human is reading it. This is not to say that Rakosi has explained away or made sense of our condition, but that he has sought to witness both the self and the world, as it were, religiously.

> The word *reverence* baffles me, for I have found nothing that I can honestly say I revere. Yet nothing touches me more deeply than that word. It has sent me a messenger in the slow grave measures of music, and in the silences between.[16]

5 Lorine Niedecker: Light and Silence

In a long poem entitled "Wintergreen Ridge," published in 1969, the late Lorine Niedecker wrote:

> Nobody　　nothing
> 　ever gave me
> 　　greater thing
>
> than time
> 　unless light
> 　　and silence
>
> which if intense
> 　makes sound[1]

It was only shortly before her death that a collection of thirty years of work, approximately fifty pages of occasions when she deemed the light and silence intense enough, was published under the title *T & G: The Collected Poems (1936–1966)*. This book, along with a somewhat overlapping selection entitled *North Central*, brought her an audience beyond the circle of poets who had read and appreciated her work. Her obscurity, aided by a diffidence which is as personal as it is poetic in her work, made her, of all the Objectivist poets, the least known.

Nevertheless, her involvement stems from the Objectivist movement's earliest days.

Although Niedecker's work was not included in either the Objectivist issue of *Poetry* or in Zukofsky's anthology, and even though she lived much of her adult life in rural Wisconsin, Niedecker maintained a career-long connection with Zukofsky. Zukofsky was mentor, friend, advisor and critic, as well as a conduit to the publications and theorizing of the other Objectivist poets, in a relationship that spanned nearly fifty years of Niedecker's creative life. Zukofsky included her poetry in his *A Test of Poetry* in 1948, and her "public" identification with the Objectivists came in the 1950s and 1960s when her work appeared in Cid Corman's *Origin* magazine, which, at that time, published much of Zukofsky's major work.

In Niedecker, the force of the Objectivist principles of sincerity and objectification is in a way as directly related to the ear's capacity for registration as in the work of Zukofsky. Niedecker's work, pointedly framed around the situations of her life and her intense, often quirky readings in history and philosophy, was an attempt to render the music of the personal occasion; in this, it varies considerably from the public and epistemological concerns of Oppen or Rakosi. At the same time, what her poems lose by the conscious shunning of large-scale civic subject matter, they gain in a remarkable intensity. In reading Niedecker, one is drawn immediately into the poem as a finished or accomplished, yet highly personalized utterance. The poet's voice possesses the reader; he is denied the balanced tone and refusal to judge that is, for example, Reznikoff's most obvious quality. Indeed, of all the Objectivists, Niedecker's work most closely resembles the "singability" that is everywhere apparent in Zukofsky's poems.

Niedecker's poems most clearly correspond to Zukofsky's theorizing concerning sound in poetry. In "A Statement for Poetry," Zukofsky formulates the following: "(The poet) looks, so to speak, into his ear as he does at the same time his heart and intellect. His ear is sincere if his words convey his awareness of

the range of differences and subtleties of duration."[2] The no-
tion here of "sincere," the Objectivist formulation of sincerity,
has an ethical weight, connoting a willingness to stand by one's
word and one's work, to be "true" in a sense to one's situation.*
In Niedecker, the "sincere" aspect of her work lies in its music,
in the way pitch and tone are derived with immense precision
from syllable and word, and in the tensed cadence in which
they are employed, in the "objectification" of the music, so to
speak. This musicality is rooted in the word choice and dic-
tion—the rhetorical or emotional claims the ostensible subject
of the poem might make on a reader are, in this sense, of a
secondary nature. If this is true of all good poems, in Niedeck-
er's work, the fusion of sound and meaning acquires such ob-
jectified solidity that critical exegesis and paraphrasing are nearly
impossible. Thus, in Niedecker, as in Zukofsky, we are meant
to take note of every element of sound, sense, and punctua-
tion. Such notice, forced upon the reader by the spare craft
and lack of "ideas," gives to Niedecker's poems an allusive mys-
teriousness, as in these carefully weighted lines from *T & G*:

> What bird would light
> in a moving tree
> the tree I carry
> for privacy?
> Down in the grass
> the question's inept[3]

Here the exact intonation of "privacy"—in this case, bell-like
and drawn out—depends upon a compilation of echoing sounds
in the "v" in "moving" and the "a" and "y" in "carry," and on
the rising effect of the question mark (which also acts as a bridge
to the word "Down" in the following line). The tonal effect,
suggesting both longing and ambivalence, strikes the ear as a
powerful oddity because it contrasts so sharply with the typical
curtness of the expression (as in "I want my privacy"). The

---

*Objectivist sincerity in this connection is deeply informed by Pound's read-
ing of Confucius.

effect saturates the image of the moving tree, transforming it from a shield against others into an emblem of the poet's lonely vulnerability. The mysteriousness of the poem is partly created by the symbolic use of tree—posed in the image as broomlike, sweeping sky to catch something as much as to ward it off. But this ambiguity of symbol is equally achieved in the way "privacy" sounds, almost in opposition to its lexical meaning. One is convinced by such a poem primarily through one's hearing, and in this, Niedecker's work is correlative with the short lyrics of Sappho or Dickinson or with the dense modalities of lyricism found in the Greek Anthology.

Niedecker's poems are for the most part notations of isolation, of the poet's own and her world's sheer recalcitrance, a record of an inert and almost blind physicality which she confronts in both her native landscape, the rural Midwest, and in its people, "the folk from whom all poetry flows / and dreadfully much else."[4] The poems strike the reader as natural and seemingly artless constructions, as artless as the region they mirror, a part of the United States, plowed and grazed but as yet unhumbled by technology. It is out of this austerity of place and out of her loneliness that Niedecker speaks, creating a poetry of resolutions and accommodations, as in the following passage from *T & G*:

> These men are our woods
> yet I grieve.
>
> I'm swamp
> as against a large pine-spread—
> his clear No marriage
> no marriage
> friend.[5]

Niedecker's craft seems aimed at conveying this unmediated impact of her experience, of adhering to Zukofsky's dictum that it is "impossible to communicate anything but particulars." In Niedecker, this particularization, worded rather than painted or photographed and thus having music of its own, becomes a sound cue leading the poet toward deeper levels of penetration and richness, as in this extremely short poem from *T & G*:

> Hear
> where her snow grave is
> the *You*
>   *ah you*
> of mourning doves.[6]

Niedecker placed such poems as this under the general title "In Exchange for Haiku." This title is suggestive, for the poem not only displays a haiku-like compression but reworks the haiku's immediacy of comparison on the level of punned or shadowed tone. Thus, the "Hear" above carries the word "here" in the same way that the dove's cry carries the word "you." Human (poet) and non-human (buried loved one and bird) seem to communicate by means of this tonal symmetry, which subsumes the referent quality of the words within the music.

The self-containment, the "economy of presentation," to use Zukofsky's phrase, gives Niedecker's poems a nodal or atom-like quality. They seem to appear out of nowhere, require no particular version of the world to sustain their effects. They follow out Niedecker's intentions, as she once wrote, of "planting poems in deep silence."[7] The silence surrounds them, giving them the requisite "objectification"; they stand with, as well as within, the material world like the "durable works / in creation here"[8] which she compares to poetry in "Wintergreen Ridge."

This materiality makes even her most painful poems seem neither self-pitying nor mean. For there is in Niedecker's work an obstinacy, an almost iron commitment to valuing her world, a moral concern for her art that is both rare and impressive. It is a concern for clarity, for the most basic knowing of one's existence; it manifests itself in the poetry with the force of Zukofsky's phrase "in sincerity." Thus, in poem after poem, Niedecker seeks to establish precisely how it is that a human suffers and celebrates the existence of other humans, other objects in the world. Craft becomes synonymous with "sincerity" here as it seeks for full knowledge or—which is the same thing—full examination. One can see this sense of craft at work in one of her early poems:

> There's a better shine
> on the pendulum
> than is on my hair
> and many times
>
> . .   . .
>
> I've seen it there.[9]

Here, the attentive silence, the pause between the last two lines, ingathers the poet's feelings of jealousy and love of beauty so that the line "I've seen it there" can bear witness to both feelings, a witnessing which, if it took sides, would be absurd or banal. The poem illustrates how a power is derived not from human vanity or longing but from an objective disclosure, an ability to render with exactness the totality of a subjective relationship.

With Niedecker, to render, to create such summations, is to do more than substantiate one's own existence; it is to create through craft a dialectic of words and silences with which the reader can interact, as in the following poem written for Zukofsky's young son, Paul:

> Paul
>   when the leaves
>   fall
> from their stems
>   that lie thick
>   on the walk
>   in the light
>   of the full note
>   the moon
> playing

> to leaves
>   when they leave
> the little
>   thin things
>   Paul[10]

As with all of Niedecker's poetry, the experience of passing
through this poem is mainly sensuous. Moving across and down
the lines, one encounters neither ideas nor statements but
complex musical interplays: rising and dying sounds, imagery
as much counterpoint as counterpart to the music. Such ten-
sions and delays function to build the poem into its own justi-
fication and release: an articulation of no more than its means,
discharging all the energy of the poet's perceptions, yet never
driving the reader out of relation to the poem.

This musical dialectic, however, relies precariously on the
good faith of both poet and reader; though palpably sounded,
the poem is free of rhetorical flourish, in the service of Nie-
decker's remark to Cid Corman that "I'd rather *say* than
write. . . ."[11] The poems, then, are made with such strictness,
such rigor to say no more than what must be said—Niedecker
humorously called her work "a condensary"—that they are
less in danger of being misunderstood than overlooked.

This is to trust one's language—today a decidedly uncom-
mon virtue—as an occasion in which a "world" might occur, in
which "a weedy speech / a marshy retainer"[12] sustains a life or
at least offers definition to its isolations. Thus, Niedecker relies
on the fiercest, simplest powers of ordinary words, those words,
as Freud put it, in which the sum total of magic is reposited.
In this she is a true keeper of the word-hoard, repurifying its
contents through scrupulous use, reawakening in her readers
the sheer dignity of human utterance.

Such a scrupulosity, however, should not be mistaken for
modesty or restraint; rather, it locates usage in necessity, cre-
ates a poetry, to use Roland Barthes' term of "a possible adven-
ture: the meeting point of a sign and an intention." For Nie-
decker, the courageous intention is to experience the world as

it is, to arrive disarmed but for her language. Thus, her poems are free of conceptions and prefigurations; they seem, in their way, to be without intellectual means, often appearing as artless as this poem from *T & G*:

> Who was Mary Shelley?
> what was her name
> before she married?
> She eloped with this Shelley
> she rode a donkey
> till the donkey had to be carried.
> Mary was Frankenstein's creator
> his yellow eye
> before her husband was to drown
> Created the monster nights
> after Byron, Shelley
> talked the candle down.
> Who was Mary Shelley?
> She read Greek, Italian
> She bore a child
> who died
> and yet another child
> who died.[13]

In the above, the nature of an identity, a "named" so to speak, is defined as its givens, a pitiless analogue of its own history, and Niedecker's collected works can be said to amount to a similar analogue. The "art" of the Mary Shelley poem is that the poem becomes a psychic vacuum which the reader is compelled to fill—a space won from fact to empathize in, to come to terms with the tragic irreducibility of the poem's last four lines. In this manner, the "deep silence," the unfilled space of the Niedecker poem, becomes the ground on which the emotions can be experienced.

Pain, loss, difficulty—these elements of failure and bitterness recur throughout the work, but Niedecker does not seek to accept failure but to reckon its cost. In one fragment she acknowledges:

> My life is hung up
> in the flood
> a wave-blurred
> portrait
> Don't fall in love
> with this face—
> it no longer exists[14]

But the reckoning is imaginative; its precision, its limitedness and finitude are in the service of the artistic dimension that can redeem one from indifferent or redundant fate. It strives for a difficult and courageous beauty requiring one to stay open to hurt and at the same moment to subject oneself to an almost classical scrutiny, as in the following poem from *T & G*:

> What horror to awake at night
> and in the dimness see the light
> Time is white
> mosquitoes bite
> I've spent my life on nothing.
> The thought that stings.[15]

Yet Niedecker—and this is what makes her work distinguished—has not become the poet-victim of her condition, but its agency, singing the song of her world and herself through herself. This is an objective yet human magic, one which makes her poems seem as organic as the experiences they arise from, resonating with pure being rather than associations. It is as though the linguistic act had been forced into an ultimate and concrete embrace of reflection, creating an inviolable structure that could hold the transitory, the evanescent, in a perpetually alive form.

> Remember my little granite pail?
> The handle of it was blue
> Think what's got away in my life—
> Was enough to carry me thru.[16]

That such self-examination never seems merely personal or oppressive is immaculate artistry. Niedecker's work, while never relying on any of our contemporary mythologies, seems to have the capacity to make, out of the representations of one's memory, the clean outlines of a myth. As poem-maker, Niedecker sought for the events of her life an absolute justice of words, a supra-literalness of the self which can transform existence (and this is its tragedy) into judgment.

Out of an isolation both personal and literary, Niedecker bravely breached her own reticence to speak simply and accurately, as few poets do today. Thus, despite their often bitter quality, her poems are peculiarly consoling to the reader, for they offer, above all, the comfort of substance, of authentic possession, the registration of a life that

took a lifetime
to weep
a deep
trickle[17]

6 The Modernity of Charles Reznikoff

In Aristotle's *Rhetoric* there is an interesting passage—a somewhat provocative passage perhaps from the standpoint of twentieth-century writing—which suggests that style is required of an author not so much to make an art but because one has to pierce the minds of a corrupted audience, and that it is through devices of style that such an audience can hear what an author has to say.[1] If, today, a poet's audience is limited to other poets or to the echoes, the mandatory pressures of tradition and one's peers, then the corruption or even innocence of a reading public would seem to be a minor factor in developing one's style. At the moment it seems that poets, poetry, and other serious writing go on their merry way, comfortably insulated from the dangers of communicating to the public. Who is "corrupt" in the present state of affairs—audience or poets—is a tantalizing question.

Against this backdrop, it is instructive to contemplate the work of the late Charles Reznikoff, for what is, initially, most apparent about his work is its accessibility, its sheer readability. The audience at which Reznikoff's poetry seems aimed need have no corruptions of the literary sort. The formal qualities of his work make it appealing not only to poets but to general readers as well. Yet its apparent directness, unclouded by the wars of literary modernism, is also its most subtle and most modern aspect.

In Reznikoff, we find a certain absence of style, at least of the high modernist style we have come to expect in contemporary poetry. At a glance, Reznikoff's work seems artless, artless, in contemporary terms, in the following ways: instead of modernist discontinuity there is continuity; in place of reliance on symbol and metaphor there is realistic, almost photographic precision of language.

Of all the poets loosely gathered under the "Objectivist" label coined by Zukofsky for Harriet Monroe's *Poetry* magazine in 1931, none seems to have been quite as "objective" as Reznikoff. In Reznikoff, legal training and the moral imperative of the Jew as historical witness combine with the Objectivist and Imagist principles, which guided such writers as Williams and Zukofsky, to produce a body of poetry distinguished by its clarity, judgment and tact. This notion of witness or bystander, of someone who is at the scene of events but not part of the events themselves, is implicit in all of Reznikoff's work. Volume titles such as *By the Waters of Manhattan, Testimony, Separate Ways, Going to and Fro, By the Well of Living and Seeing* are indicative of a poetic stance that was to be, as Reznikoff once put it, "content at the periphery of such wonder."[2] This "wonder" was to embrace the urban experience, in particular its relation to the life of newly immigrant Jews, as well as such topics as early Jewish history, legal proceedings in nineteenth- and twentieth-century America and the Holocaust of European Jewry.

Reznikoff's stance is not concerned so much with a conventional sense of poetic distance or with irony per se but with precision of realization. The modern city, the source of much of Reznikoff's most memorable work, is for him a place one continually passes through, a locus of large anonymous forces encountered tangentially, yet overshadowing and overwhelming the experience of the city inhabitant. The truths of the city are multiple, highly individualized, and, in Reznikoff, are caught not as part of some grand design but as minor resistances to its forces. Victories and defeats occur not in the towers of commerce or in the offices of governments, but in street-corner and kitchen tableaux in which individual fate is registered. The poems hover on the edge of factual materiality with few gestures toward the literary. Yet their construction has a cleanliness and freshness found in few other contemporaries. One goes to Reznikoff's work, not only for its poetic beauty, its surety of language, but also for its depiction of our recent history.

This "nonliterary" use of language characterizes all of Reznikoff's work. His poems strike the reader almost as a form of low-key reportage, making use of proselike speech rhythms and barely discernible shifts in discourse from statement to simile or metaphor.

In Reznikoff, the poem attains to the condition of the photograph rather than the lyric—the photograph, in the words of Walter Benjamin, as "the posthumous moment," the moment rescued from time. In Reznikoff's work, the uttered image is something other than a symbol; it becomes a window framing actual particularities and occasions, realized so authentically that they resonate with an enormous life of associations beyond the image's frame. This preciseness of realization, at root a refusal to sentimentalize its subject matter, makes of Reznikoff, among other things, our quintessential urban poet. Through his work we come to know a certain life intimately, a history, usage, custom, even religious and exalted moments, with barely a rhetorical gesture. This objective mastery, apparent from the very beginning of his work (there is little in Reznikoff's work which could be called "youthful"), has produced a body of poems remarkable for the unobtrusive manner in which they operate. Thus, in a poem from 1920:

> Suddenly we noticed that we were in darkness
> So we went into the house and lit the lamp
> And sat around, dark spaces about a sun[3]

or, more wittily, from 1969:

> Clap hands and slap your thighs;
> Adding indulgence to indulgence, sin to sin,
> the thread of the spider becomes a rope[4]

there is a reticence which has less to do with modesty than with accurate registration, metaphor being made so much a part of the observation that we hardly notice the shift in the level of discourse.

This shorn-down language simultaneously inhabits a number of linguistic realms at once; the datum and its meaning for the poet are so inextricably linked that the usual suspension of belief or accounting for poetic license no longer applies. The poetry has about it a "documentary" effect, one that is both tactful and powerful by virtue of its being stripped, it would seem, of any attempt by the poet to persuade. Such effects, by their very understatement, can achieve incredible reflexive power, as in the ending of a poem about a man who sacrifices himself for his parents and suddenly, with both dead, in his middle age, finds himself free.

> . . . To do what? He knew no one who he cared
> to marry. And who would go into his poverty?

> If he were to give up this work which he knew
> so well, to what else could he turn?

> He would just keep on. He had lost this world
> And knew there was no other.[5]

This simultaneity of judgment and tact is a form of humility, a desire that "we," as Reznikoff notes, "whose lives are only a few words" meet in the thing seen and not in the personality of the seer.

In Reznikoff, one senses a swimming against the literary current, a way of writing which seems to turn our "advances" in poetry on their heads. And yet there is certainly nothing in

Reznikoff's writing or in his relation to poetry which could suggest that he ever set any such revolutionary task for himself; the last thing to be found in Reznikoff is a desire to be original.

Whatever Reznikoff has accomplished of a literary nature—and it is that nature that I am dealing with here, thus emphasizing Reznikoff's importance as a poet rather than as a social documentor of city life, of Jewish life, and so forth—this accomplishment seems to have occurred *en passant*; it is, to put it simply, something of a toss-off. Reznikoff, it strikes me, aims at presenting a world and not literature.

The remarkable thing is how Reznikoff's world stands by itself, not because it is familiar but because it is so palpable and nuanced, so fundamentally nonliterary in character. It is as though its creator, while seeking at all costs to avoid the appearance of producing a verbal artifact, has achieved in the work those qualities of independence and autonomy that the verbal artifact aspires to. Furthermore, content and form seem completely wedded, an authentic, to use one of Roland Barthes' terms, writing degree zero, in that the residue of authorship is barely discernible. This is the *literary* meaning of Reznikoff's work, and it is this literary quality in the poetry which is as deeply moving as the humane content.

At the center of Reznikoff's writing, concomitant with the objectivity of his technique, with seeing for oneself, is the aloneness of the moral witness, a solitude which has little to do with the "alienation" normally ascribed to Jewish writers. In Reznikoff, this isolation seems less a product of experience than of insistence and fundamental choice. As he says in "Autobiography: New York":

> I am alone—
> and glad to be alone;
>
> . . . .
>
> I like the sound of the street—
> but I, apart and alone,

> beside an open window
> and behind a closed door.[6]

It is a choice going back to a deeper set of traditions, traditions embedded in Jewish religious and philosophical themes, and their influence can be felt not only in the content of much of Reznikoff's poetry but also in its form. For his work displays an attitude toward language which is close to (and may well be derived from) the Kabbalists, those compilers and annotators of the Jewish mystical tradition who, as the scholar Gershom Scholem noted in *Major Trends of Jewish Mysticism*, "revel in objective description" and who feel that language "reflects the fundamental spiritual nature of the world." There is, in Reznikoff, an awe and wonder at the power of language.

> I have learnt the Hebrew blessing before eating bread
> Is there no blessing before reading Hebrew?[7]

There is also a belief in its revelatory powers. As he affirms in one poem about the eighteenth century Jewish mystic Luzzatto:

> The sentences we studied are rungs upon the ladder Jacob saw
> The law itself is nothing but the road.[8]

Another influence is Reznikoff's early legal training, which not only contributed to his ethical sense of the witness but also formed the basis for the rigorous precision of his writing. As he relates of his law school days:

> I found it delightful . . .
> to use words for their daylight meaning
> and not as prisms
> playing with the rainbows of connotation[9]

No other poet, with perhaps the exception of Williams, has more thoroughly refused the artifices of style and chosen to let words have "their daylight meanings," to speak, first of all, humanely and communicatively.

Reznikoff's restraint before the possibilities of language seems at once spiritually felt and, paradoxically, modern. It approaches that condition Barthes has described where "the adoption of a real language is for the writer the most human act," human because it continually points at truth and at the recalcitrance of truth.

In Reznikoff, the first or primary impetus is to communicate. As the short collection of Reznikoff's prose statements *First, there is the Need* (Sparrow 52) makes clear, craft and technique stem from communicative (nearly ethical) needs as opposed to literary or formalistic concerns.

With any writer, craft suggests not only the writer's way of thought, his or her way of organizing experience, but also the writer's relation to his milieu. Reznikoff began to publish his work in 1918 and within a few years of that time gave up the traditionalist devices of fixed meter and rhyme then already under attack from Ezra Pound's and T. S. Eliot's modernism. Yet Reznikoff was not to traffic in the obviously unconventional or extreme writing of the early twentieth-century avant-garde. Even the Imagist movement, which certainly influenced Reznikoff and to which he pays homage, was refined and transmuted by him into something that would not be particularly recognizable to the founders of the movement. For the "image" of the Imagists was something decidedly literary, something used for its allusive or symbolic effect, whereas in Reznikoff, as mentioned above, it becomes a construction, one made out of observation and precise detail, concerned primarily with rendering a datum.

It is through this rendering (and here we are dealing with Reznikoff's thought) that the contents of his poetry are given their extraordinary form. For in Reznikoff, lives, cityscapes, testimonies, tend to remain resolutely what they are, to resist being read analogically or metaphorically.

Particularly in the urban poetry, there is a sealed character to the contents of the work, one that is full of sorrow, of a judging sorrow and tenderness which understands personality, even that of fools and villains, and yet accepts. In many of the poems, there seems to exist an air of resignation, a curious resignation, because in the way the contents of a poem are rendered, this atmosphere arises from its subject and not from its author's attitudes.

This air has as much to do with craft as with feeling. For what Reznikoff's work evokes—and this is its most contemporary aspect—is the perception and the humanity of the reader. The surer, possibly harsher aspects of judgment are left to the reader as if to say, let him or her decide what to feel (or do) about modern life, about the modern world. Instead of judgment, there is a sense of great detachment, a kind of moral spaciousness that the reader must cross. It is not that there are gaps of information—everything is given. Yet, as with few other contemporary bodies of verse, the reader must discover in himself the attitudes he has toward the material.

Nothing seems so aesthetically right, so convincing as this distance. We often find in Reznikoff the sense of the poet having just withdrawn from the scene of the poem, of the people themselves already in some state of taking leave. The great, the impersonal forces of city life or of history have just happened, and now there is the moment and its urging to seek stillness, a stillness in which an intuition or perception of what has occurred can take place. At times, particularly in those poems which record the experience of living in the Jewish urban ghettos of the early 1900s, there is a stifling, pervasive claustrophobia: the boy who sneaks out late at night to use his sled, fearful of being assaulted for his Jewishness in the daytime; the young woman trapped and inarticulate before the sexual advances of the foreign boarder upon whose money the family is dependent; the cello heard through the wall by a young man whose family insists that he defer and defer again his study of music. The great anxiety of city life, of things going on behind one's back, that one is essentially left out or that reasons for what has happened to one are not to be found in this life—these themes are nowhere presented more effectively than in Reznikoff.

Again, it is as much craft as content which produces the

effect. The reader is made to feel the flow of events go by, to participate only as a witness. There are no imperial gestures in the language, barely an attempt to explain, let alone interpret. This restrained use of language marks Reznikoff's entire corpus. Typical are these examples, one from 1919, which seems at first mere photographic juxtaposition:

> Stubborn flies buzzing
> in the morning when she wakes.
>
> The flat roofs, higher, lower,
> chimneys, water-tanks, cornices.
>
> (#6, Rhythms II)[10]

the other from 1969, a chilling look at the "Death of an Insect":

> The sparrow with its beak taps the beetle
> and it begins to buzz loudly
> as if the bird had set off an alarm-clock,
>
> The beetle flies off into the air
> in a series of clumsy gyrations
> and the sparrow follows it gracefully.[11]

Observation alone is, of course, not poetry; language is poetry, and in these two examples, it is an almost sleight of hand with the words "stubborn," "higher," "lower" and, in the second poem, "alarm-clock," "clumsy" and "gracefully," which transforms these words into poems. Yet they remain virtually unobtrusive rhetorical gestures, words almost submerged in the subject, partaking of the thing observed.

This poetic technique, which Reznikoff called "recitative," stresses the evidential or communicative aspect of language over the figurative; it unites all of Reznikoff's work, from the early *Rhythms* published in 1918 up to and through the late volumes of *Testimony* and *Holocaust*. The minimal use of poetic devices such as rhyme, metaphor or exaggerated imagery results in a restrained tone that balances irony, sarcasm and humor with emotional distance. It is particularly apt for the short two or three-line poem (one of Reznikoff's trademarks) which combines a wise knowingness with bleak hilarity, as in "permit me to warn you / against this automobile rushing to embrace you / with outstretched fender."[12] It also attains a meditative strength, as in "among the heaps of brick and plaster lies / a girder, still itself among the rubbish."[13] Here, the double reading of "still itself" transforms the poem from mere description to enigmatic philosophy.

Such surety of technique makes Reznikoff's poems radiate with both completeness of finish *and* mystery, as though their author, while knowing much, says little. Indeed, they sustain an aphoristic or epigrammatic tone, even in poems of great length, covering a wide variety of subject matter.

A similar process is at work in those poems which comment on or make use of biblical and talmudic material. Here we find the use of personae or present-tense narration conveying immediacy to the work, yet at the same time distancing the reader. In these poems, Reznikoff's "recitative" becomes a recital, one which has the authenticity of an unearthed text and yet the freshness of contemporary language. This, for example, is an excerpt from *Jews in Babylonia*:

> The dead woman has forgotten her comb
> and tube of eye-paint;
> the dead cobbler has forgotten his knife,
> the dead butcher his chopper,
> and the dead carpenter his adze.
>
> A goat can be driven off with a shout.
> But where is the man to shout?
> The bricks pile up, the laths are trimmed,
> and the beams are ready. Where is the builder?
>
> To be buried in a linen shroud
> or matting of reeds—
> but where are the dead of the Flood
> and where are the dead of Nebuchadnezzar?[14]

Now, as Reznikoff's few prose comments on his poetry make clear, craft and technique stem for him from communicative and ethical concerns, as opposed to literary ones, and it is this urge to communicate which is his primary motive. One finds in his work that nearly lost sense of the poet as reteller of tales, as tribal historian. The poet, according to Reznikoff (perhaps in particular the Jewish poet of the People of the Book) stands always with history at his back. For such a poet, the work is not one of self-expression but one of a desire to speak for those voices lost or denied in time, for individuals caught up in historical forces beyond their control. But this urge to reclaim has deeper implications in Reznikoff. This is clearly demonstrated in another section of *Jews in Babylonia*, where a collagist technique initially yokes natural phenomena, the passing of seasons, the growth of plants, the behavior of animals, with simple actions of the biblical tradesmen: "Plane the wood into boards; chisel the stone." The rhythms here are stately and the imagery peaceful. But as the poem continues, this harmony begins to come apart. Now there is "a beast with its load / and a bit in its mouth" and "the horn gores / the hoof kicks / the teeth bite." The shift in tone becomes even more "unnatural": "The bread has become moldy / and the dates blown down by the wind." This line is followed by the passage quoted above with its endings in a litany of ruin and decay which has both historical and metaphysical implications, as sounded in the lines "but where are the dead of the Flood . . . the dead of Nebuchadnezzar?" Finally the recital of images begins to express a kind of visionary chaos where "the hyena will turn into a bat / and a bat will turn into a thorn," where what is seen is "the blood of his wounds / and the tears of her eyes" and "the Angel of Death in time of war / does not distinguish / between the righteous and the wicked." The effect of this technique is to create something that seems at once cinematic and apocalyptic, forcefully in keeping with the historical situation itself, while at the same time suggesting both foreboding and prophecy. In this regard, Reznikoff's work is no simple addition to or nostalgic reminder of the past but, like the songs and poems of the biblical prophets, a potential guide to personal and social action. As he says of his grandfather's lost poetry in "By the Well of Living and Seeing": "All the verse he wrote was lost— except for what / still speaks through me / as mine." Such poetry seems to resonate in two worlds at once: the historical and the imaginative. As with the shopkeepers and apartment dwellers of Reznikoff's urban poetry, who labor under the city's impersonal forces, the poem above recapitulates, and so honors, the deaths of history's minor characters who are caught up in nationalistic and religious struggles beyond their control.

The intention of these poems, it must be insisted on, has nothing to do with a suspension of judgment or with the shallow themes of artistic and moral relativism which seem to be in fashion today. On the contrary: Reznikoff's intention is to provide the occasion for accurate understanding and judgment. In this regard, his long relationship with the law, with legal proceedings and lawyers, and its effect on his poetry are not only technical but moral. As he comments in *First, there is the Need*:

> With respect to the treatment of subject matter in verse and the use of the term "objectivist" and "objectivism," let me again refer to the rules with respect to testimony in a court of law. Evidence to be admissable in a trial cannot state conclusions of fact: it must state the facts themselves. For example, a witness in an action for negligence cannot say: the man injured was negligent in crossing the street. He must limit himself to a description of how the man crossed: did he stop before crossing? Did he look? Did he listen? The *conclusions* (my italics) of fact are for the jury and let us add, in our case, for the reader.[15]

In such works as *Holocaust* and *Testimony*, the refinement of Reznikoff's method reaches an austere and heightened level. These works, edited from court testimony, trial records and historical documents, seem at first to be what we have come to call "found poems" (if such material in its sheer poetic recalcitrance can be called poetry). For it is the selection and arrangement alone, that is, the fact that they are versed, sectioned and placed in book form, that indicate that these are to be taken as poems. Yet the author's relation to the materials is not to be discovered except in their *presentness*.* The total burden of interpretation appears to be left to the reader; there is, by usual standards, nothing of literary value, nothing quotable or memorable, or even ironic—indeed, irony, in whatever form, must be supplied, as to the pedestal of Ozymandias's pillar, by the affected reader. Shorn of entertainment value, of sentiment, this work seems to place a curious demand on the modern reader. And yet that these poems are simultaneously a witnessing and a rejecting of any social, artistic or psychological agenda in their presentation, that these materials are able to "speak for themselves," strikes the reader as not only proper but in some powerful way as noble.

Thus, in commanding response but not dictating it, Reznikoff manages to give both good and bad conscience their due. This, of course, is modernity with a vengeance. For here, the "poetic" by its very absence in the poetry seems to be both witness and prosecutor, reminder to the reader not only of the events that have occurred but of the life and possibility denied by the events. The works curiously penetrate the reader's consciousness since, by leaving all to individual interpretation, they undermine, in their account of devastating cruelty and horror, the reader's conventional notions of civilization and culture.

Such penetration, accomplished in such a 'hands off' manner, has the further effect of evoking and calling to account the reader's humanity. It is this effect which gives Reznikoff's "objectivity" such moral power. This wedding of artistic means and the procedures of the law courts gives to Reznikoff's work a unique contemporaneity, one which honors and respects the individual, while in no way striving for egocentric novelty. This

---

*Milton Hindus, in his moving critical essay "Charles Reznikoff," discusses in detail the way Reznikoff expunged, in revision after revision, all hint of authorial intent. Hindus's book-length study, published by Black Sparrow not long after Reznikoff's death, is the most thoroughgoing introduction to Reznikoff's life and work now available.

is a *communitas* at its most moving and profound. It can be said of Reznikoff that he is one of the few poets of our time to have transformed literary artistry into a major historical vision.

Artistic resolution and legal judgment are by no means synonymous, yet both aim at a kind of wholeness which is intellectually and psychologically satisfying. This satisfaction in works of art is always mysterious because our views, our understanding of events and of our worlds, are always partial, never exhaustive. Reznikoff's stylistic restraint has the effect of leaving the subjects of his poetry, like the things of the phenomenal world, with their intactness preserved, their tacit being untouched. Whatever their personal value to him, it is in this relentless pursuit of their being that Reznikoff's craft and subtlety are expressed. The paradox of Reznikoff's work, its modernity so to speak, is that the specific and the concrete, in their very limitedness, are the gates to wholeness. In Reznikoff, this limitedness becomes but the other side of openness and generosity towards experience. Through it we are uncompromisingly reminded that we have hearts and minds of our own, that we too are the witnesses of our world.

This power in Reznikoff to invoke the humanity of the reader seems ultimately in the service of prophecy and vision. Like the Old Jew of *In Memoriam* its meaning is to

> strengthen ourselves
> in struggling with our father's foes, long nameless
> and merely the people of our thoughts—
> .... some day ready to act again—[16]

At times mordant and witty, at times grave, Reznikoff's work achieves that vantage between the objective and the subjective worlds, between instruction and pleasure, that is the mark of moral vision.

> Do not mourn the dandelions—
> that their golden heads become grey
> in no time at all

and are blown about in the wind;
each season shall bring them again to the lawns;
but how long the seeds of justice
stay underground
how much blood and ashes of precious things
to manure so rare and brief a growth.[17]

I submit: we are in great need of so rare and precious a vision.

7 The Mind of George Oppen: Conviction's Net of Branches

In one of George Oppen's poems, the poet is being driven around an island off the coast of Maine by a poor fisherman and his wife. The landscape, the lobster pots and the fishing gear, the harbor and the post office are passed, and the poet is, unaccountably, moved by a nearly metaphysical sense of passage. The experience is at once intimate and remote, and the poet is moved to exclaim to himself "difficult to know what one means / —to be serious and to know what one means—."[1] Such lines could be emblems for all of Oppen's entire career; for of all contemporary poets, none has more searchingly investigated, through poetry, the attempt to mean, to examine how language is used and thus to account for the very vocabulary of our modernity. Oppen's poetry can be said to be one of our most sustained examinations of the characteristic themes of poetry (themes of love and death, and of a sense of history), an attempt to determine if the very meaning of such words as "love" or "humanity" can be retained in the light of what we have come to know and of what we have become. Indeed, Oppen's work has been to show forth the meanings of these terms by exploring, in the deepest sense, our need to resort to them.

Oppen sees the poet involved in a task which is as much question and inquiry as it is an order of expression, a task which asks whether the moral, religious and philosophical notions by which we live, and which have formed our common heritage, are any longer possibilities. Oppen's poetry arises from our own ambivalence toward what we know and have come to rely on. It is marked by an awareness of the human effort to remain in predictive and utilitarian certainties—an awareness also of the religious attractiveness they engender. Yet the power of his poems is that they do deliver us, by a process of skeptical homage, into a world seen afresh, vivified by an avoidance of inauthentic and outworn sentiment.

There are certain pressures and attitudes in what we might call the Western mind with which Oppen has been struggling throughout his career. There is that impulse, which for better or worse is labeled "metaphysical," that taste

> for bedrock
> Beneath this spectacle
> To gawk at . . .
> (from "The Taste," *Seascape: Needle's Eye*)[2]

At the same time, Oppen is concerned with the contrary of that taste, the hardening of what is intellectually and emotionally grasped into conceptions, into a "Solution," as Oppen ironically entitled an early poem about a jigsaw puzzle "assembled at last," which curiously apes our flawed science and technology.

> The jigsaw of cracks
> Crazes the landscape but there is no gap
> No actual edged hole
> Nowhere the wooden texture of the table top
> Glares out of scale in the picture,
> Sordid as cellars, as bare foundations:
> There is no piece missing. The puzzle is complete
> Now in its red and green and brown.
> (from *The Materials*)[3]

The irony here of course is that in addition to its freight of misused benefits and dangling hopes, this "solution" too, by virtue of that metaphysical impulse, begins to look like—to use a recurrent and important expression of Oppen's—"mechanics," or "remote mechanics" as he says in one poem. The expression has less to do with the rampant technology of modern life than with the perception that our inventions and solutions seem to lie at some distance from a human world. Oppen's poetry, far from offering yet another solution, seems to be asking whether human beings have the capacity to dwell any longer in what Keats defined as "negative capability," to live, that is, without the need for heavy reference points disguised in theological and political systems.

Oppen's entire body of work can be seen as a modern test of the poet's capacity to articulate. The terms of his poetry are the common meanings of words as they attempt to render the brute givens of the world of appearance. For this reason, Oppen has called his work "realist," realist in the sense that it is "concerned with a fact (the world) which it did not create."[4] In a way, the subject of all of Oppen's poetry is the nature of this encounter with the world or with others. According to Oppen, the task for the poet is not to sentimentally beautify or categorize such encounters but to render their living quality, to make the poet's relatedness to the facts into something felt, even where to do so is to admit the difficulty of the task. Oppen acknowledges in one of his poems: "Perhaps one is himself / Beyond the heart, the center of the thing / and cannot praise it / As he would want to. . . ."[5] In this estrangement, poet, thinker, and contemporary man are cojoined in a time when, as the critic Erich Heller has noted in *The Disinherited Mind*, "uncertainty alone is ineluctably real."[6]

Oppen is among our most profound and eloquent explorers of this theme, profound because he comes without illusion into the act of writing poetry, eloquent because the order of his craft cannot be separated from the order of his perception. In *Seascape: Needle's Eye*, for example, his interrogation of reality in language, an interrogation which has always been at the very center of his work, is an effort, as Wittgenstein warned, against the bewitchment of language itself.

> 'out of poverty
> to begin
>
> again' impoverished
>
> of tone of pose that common
> wealth
>
> of parlance
> (from "The Winds of Downhill," *Collected Poems*)[7]

Such "poverty" provides a peculiarly modern test of articulation, a form of resolve against certain historical and elegiac associations of words and against the convenient knowingness of slang. Kenner, in *The Pound Era*, speaking of the yet to be written history of the Objectivists—among them Oppen, Williams, and Zukofsky—puts it this way: "In that machine (the poem) made of words . . . (the word) is a term, not a focus for sentiment, simply a word, the exact and plausible word, not inviting the imagination to linger; an element in the economy of a sentence."[8] In Oppen, this is a principle raised to a very high degree of thoughtfulness and choice. Indeed, in reading him, one often feels that one is confronting not so much an innovation or experiment as a search for the adequation of means and ends, an intuitive feel for what is necessary. What is given up, or, in Oppen's case, rarely taken up, is the analogical mode in language where image and symbol stand as metaphors for another reality. Because of this, Oppen's work seems like a kind of first poetry, not by virtue of any crudeness since it is both a subtle and sophisticated body of verse, but by the sheer unaccountability of its construction. Its beauty and power derive from the reader's simultaneous apperception of its radical construction and the depth at which it seeks to cohere.

In all of Oppen's work, there is an attempt to render the visual datum accurately and precisely; this is, in keeping with the Imagist and Objectivist techniques, at the root of Oppen's poetics. However, the aim of the technique is more philosophic than literary; it attempts to establish the material saliency or otherness of the visual event. In the poems, objects and landscapes obtrude and seem to reveal their existence as though seen for the first time. *Discrete Series* (published in 1934), Oppen's first book, is nearly procedural in its epistemological insistence on what is seen. The short lyrics comprised in it are less like poems than like the recording of eye-movements across surfaces which are juxtaposed against snatches of statements and remembered lines from older poetry and fiction.

> Closed car—closed in glass—
> At the curb,
> Unapplied and empty:
> A thing among others
> Over which clouds pass and the
>   alteration of lightning,
> An overstatement
> Hardly an exterior.
> Moving in traffic
> This thing is less strange—
> Tho the face still within it,
> Between glasses—place, over which
>   time passes—a false light.[9]

This poem prefigures many of the techniques which would be central to Oppen's later work. Most important of all is the reliance on the substantive or noun clause as the basis of poetic statement: the closed car of the poem, for example, is "tracked" through a philosophical as well as a physical landscape, the object accreting detail and comment in the poem until its carness and relation to humans who use it become an epiphany on time, a meditation on transitoriness and the need to project into objects our fear of death and change. Such poems—and *Discrete Series* is composed almost totally of such a kind—operate somewhat like the late, peopleless paintings of Edward Hopper in that they eerily reconstruct human anguish out of absence and a curious tangibility to the physical materials of the world. The white space of the page, like Hopper's flat yet oppressive light, surrounds the poem's elements and becomes a field of hesitations, advances and reconsiderations. The burden of meaning in the poems resides in the reader's recomposition of the fragmented elements. It is as though a crystal or diffracting prism were interspersed between the poet and the subject of the poem.

Soon after the publication of *Discrete Series*, Oppen was to give up writing poetry for nearly twenty-five years under the pressure of his Populist politics and interest in worker-related causes. By the time Oppen resumed writing poetry in the late 1950s, he had greatly modified both his sense of and reliance on the visual as a source of knowledge; yet one of the chief distinctions of his poetry remains its persuasive power of registration, as in this example from a poem written in the 1960's where "the north / Looks out from its rock / bulging into the fields,"[10] or from a poem of the 1970s, where the sun moves "beyond the blunt / towns of the coast . . . fishermen's / tumbled tumbling headlands the needle silver / water. . . ."[11] Such imagery attempts to evoke the solidity and palpability of the world, and, at the same time, to suggest its ungainliness, its obdurate self-referential quality, which contrasts sharply with our usual visual clichés.

This sense of the visual, however, is for Oppen but one element of a dialectical occasion, an occasion in which poetic truth resides neither in the object nor in the poet but in the interaction between the two. If, as Oppen would insist, the poet's ultimate aim is truth, then what is seen has the possibility of being a kind of measure: seeing precedes verbalization and therefore offers an opportunity for an open response to the world. This opportunity is, of course, hedged round with all one's conditioned reflexes, the material of which the poet must work through to arrive at a sense of the real. It is in this "working through" that Oppen's poetics, though concerned with ambiguity and paradox, strive for a clarity that is both immediate and complex, one which the reader, following the process of thought and imagery in the poem, can at least acknowledge as considered. Oppen, as noted above, has described this as an attempt to write a poetry which "cannot not be understood."

This process can be seen at work in *The Materials* of 1962, the first of Oppen's major collections to be written and published after his lengthy political and geographical hiatus from the world of poetry. The book's underlying theme, carried through its forty-one poems, is clearly signaled in its epigraph from the philosopher Jacques Maritain: "We awake in the same moment to ourselves and to things." Oppen's "subject" is these awakenings, awakenings which are capable of transcending the usual notions of self and of society. In one of the book's major poems, "Return," amidst "the dim sound of the living," the very impingement of the natural world becomes a moment in which "we cannot reconcile ourselves. / No one is reconciled, tho we spring / From the ground together—" Nor is this estrangement, so the poem continues, eased by a sense of history or community; these are fictions in their way, and to look closely at them is to feel "the sense of that passage / is desertion / betrayal, that we are not innocent / of loneliness. . . ." The poem ends with an image of the poet's old neighborhood, "razed, whole blocks / of a city gone . . . ," in which "the very ceremony of innocence" has been drowned.

In Oppen, such a loss of innocence is not to be mourned; rather, it is the very beginning of a truer relatedness between individuals, and between the individual and the world, a relatedness based on a language shorn of older, inauthentic mythologies. "Leviathan," the last poem in *The Materials*, insists that "truth also is the pursuit of it," that "we must talk now. Fear / is fear. But we abandon one another." [13]

Oppen's next book, *This in Which*, is an exploration of the nature of such "talk." Here the poet's search is for a "substantial language of clarity, and of respect," [14] a language based on a willingness to look fully, without illusion, at the human condition. It is "possible to use words," the poet tells us, "provided one treat them as enemies. / Not enemies—Ghosts which have run mad." [15] Comparing modern consciousness to that of the primitive Mayans and their mythic view of life, to "the poor savages of ghost and glitter," Oppen reminds us that it is necessary to examine squarely the "terror / the unsightly / silting sand of events." [16] Oppen's method of stripping language of its historical associations reminds us how apt Kenner's motto "No myths" is for the Objectivists. "Art," Oppen warns, following a similar line of thought, "also is not good for us / unless . . . it may rescue us / as only the true / might rescue us." [17]

These themes, of a need for a demythologizing poetics and of a language adequate to render the fullness of reality, are brought to culmination in *Of Being Numerous*, the book-length poem which many critics consider Oppen's masterpiece. *Of Being Numerous* is concerned with the deepest notions of community and with the basis on which community might be established: with the meaning of humanity, ethics and love. The poem is, in a sense, an interrogation of these terms, an attempt to discover whether these words can truthfully be retained in the light of what humanity has become.

The poem's first section speaks of "the things we live among," that "'to see them / is to know ourselves.'" [18] For these constitute, like the adrift, bereft objects of *Discrete Series*, a telling inventory. They are:

> The sad marvels;
>
> Of this was told
> A tale of our wickedness.
> It is not our wickedness.

The "marvels" are "sad" because they not only embody mankind's capacity for invention and creativity but reify, and even fetishize, hope and longing. In Oppen's purview, they are, at best, flawed indicators of self-knowledge; mostly, they are, as he notes in section two, "an unmanageable pantheon," "a city of the corporations / glassed in dreams / and images."[19] This shared world, the poem seems to suggest, is not so much the basis of our communal bonds but an expression of its failure to release humanity from its sense of solitude and dread. For Oppen, the word "community" represents, in the present, an expression of the individual's psychic needs, of the effect of anxiety on contemporary life. Hence, in Oppen's view, the very notion of community is, at best, flawed and irrational. Humanity, the poem tells us, is "bewildered / by the shipwreck / of the singular"; thus, "we have chosen the meaning / of being numerous."[20] Given this situation, how to "talk distantly of the people."[21] There is now only "a ferocious mumbling in public / of rootless speech." Against this mumbling, Oppen seeks to set forth the truth-value of poetic speech.

Such truth-value, as Oppen, and indeed the other Objectivist poets, insist, is itself discomforting, cutting through the illusions thrown up by such terms as society and nation. For these words have more to do with psychological stratagems than with defining ourselves to ourselves publicly. As Oppen says in section twenty-six:

> We want to defend
> Limitation
> And do not know how

And this defense has invaded poetic language itself, for "They" (the poets)

> . . . have lost the metaphysical sense
> Of the future, they feel themselves
> The end of a chain
>
> Of lives, single lives
> And we know that lives
> Are single
>
> And cannot defend

> The metaphysic
> On which rest
>
> The boundaries
> Of our distance.
> We want to say
>
> 'Common sense'
> And cannot. We stand on
>
> That denial
> Of death that paved the cities.[22]

For the poem, as Oppen would have us see it, must attempt, not to lull one into another false sense of community, but to clear the air of bankrupt sentimentality about community and to reestablish community on a recognition of each other's essential aloneness.

Thus, Oppen insists, that "it is difficult now to speak of poetry—,"[23] for such speaking must be based on the "isolation of the actual," on

> —such solitude as we know.
>
> One must not come to feel that he has a thousand threads
>   in his hands.
> He must somehow see the one thing;
> This is the level of art
> There are other levels
> But there is no other level of art.

Here the "level of art" is synonymous with Oppen's "test of sincerity, the moment . . . when you believe something to be true, and you construct a meaning from these moments of conviction." Section twenty-nine is a moving affirmation of such a "test":

> My daughter, my daughter, what can I say
> Of living?
>
> I cannot judge it.
>
> We seem caught

> In reality together
> My lovely daughter,
>
> I have a daughter
> But no child
>
> And it was not precisely
> Happiness we promised
> Ourselves;
>
> We say, happiness, happiness and are not
> Satisfied.
>
> Tho the house on the low land
> Of the city
>
> Catches the dawn light
>
> I can tell myself, and I tell myself
> Only what we all believe
> True[24]

In such a moment, one has, as Oppen says, "a daughter but no child," for it is only "in the sudden vacuum of time" in "fear" that

> The roots grip
>
> Downward
> And beget
>
> The baffling hierarchies
> Of father and child
>
> As of leaves on their high
> Thin twigs to shield us
>
> From time, from open
> Time

Such instances of clarity and honesty are our true connectedness, Oppen claims. For they, the poem continues, permit us to discover "not truth, but each other."[25] Such an interrogation of our human condition, and how we speak of it, does not, in

Oppen's view, lead to further despair and alienation but to a redemption of the time and place in which we live:

> Like the wind in the trees and the bells
> Of the procession—
>
> How light the air is
> And the earth,
>
> Children and the grass
> In the wind and the voices of men and women
>
> To be carried about the sun forever
>
> Among the beautiful particulars of the breeze
> The papers blown about the sidewalks . . . [26]

The poem ends with a short quote from Whitman's prose, written in admiration of the capitol building in Washington with its bronze *Genius of Liberty* mounted on top. The very last word "curious"[27] overshadows the argument of the poem, for in its admixture of creative interest and intention to witness, it gathers Oppen's many themes into that "one level of art," leading the reader to this understanding, not by rational means, but by the powerful dynamics of aesthetic response. In such a response is to be found "our jubilation / exalted and as old as that truthfulness / which illumines speech."[28]

Oppen's more recent work, beginning with *Seascape: Needle's Eye* (1972) and continuing through his latest collection, *Primitive* (1977), involves a radical departure from the poetry which came before. In the earlier poems, in particular in *Of Being Numerous*, Oppen created a restrained but rhetorically powerful amalgam of statement and imagery, a poetry, which like a Socratic dialogue, aimed at undermining conventional thought and attitude. In the new poems, the chaos and flux of life, the ever partial mythologizing that language enacts, are embodied in a troubled and moving voice, one that seems to embrace deeply the contingency and indeterminacy of life.

Throughout *Seascape: Needle's Eye*, more so than in the earlier work, there is a heightened sense of the struggle to articulate: the language is starker, more primordial, as is the use of spacing, so that the poems create a feeling of resolution arrived at only *in extremis*. Against the earlier conception of the "mechanics" of thought, Oppen poses the world of temporality and fragility, of a mutable aliveness, the tragic dimension of which is stasis and death. This encounter is experienced through sight and emotion, that "emotion which causes to see," as it is defined in an earlier poem. And it is not that one sees something unusual or novel, but that one sees unusually, attentively, with an intensity of sight* that moves

> with all one's force
> Into the commonplace that pierces or erodes
> (from "The Occurrences," *Collected Poems*)[29]

or that becomes

> Ob   via   the obvious . . .
>
> Place
> Place where desire
> Lust of the eyes the pride of life . . .
> ("From a Phrase of Simone Weil's and Some
> Words of Hegel's," *Collected Poems*)[30]

Such a passage harks back to that epigram of Heidegger's which Oppen has quoted and which might well be the rubric of all of Oppen's poetics: "The arduous path of appearance."

The world of appearance and the communality of words (their intersubjective meanings) form the twin aspects of Oppen's late poetry. The poems move as dialectical occasions between sight and naming, and the poet's truth—perhaps no one else's— is established in the encounter between what is seen and what is said, with the poet as mediating agency in the process. To this extent, the encounter is seen by Oppen as one which is

*I would refer readers to L. S. Dembo's essay "The Existential World of George Oppen" (*Denver Quarterly*) for further discussion of the importance of sight and clarity in Oppen's work.

extreme in its selflessness. Yet it is not impersonal, not a ne-
gation of personality as the word "objective" might imply; rather,
it is a going through personality, a testing of the ego.

> . . . Liquid
> Pride of the living life's liquid
> Pride in the sandspit wind this ether this other
> > this element all
>
> It is I or I believe
>
> . . . no other way
> To come here the outer
> Limit of the ego.
> > ("From a Phrase of Simone Weil's and Some
> > Words of Hegel's," *Collected Poems*)[31]

In these later poems this is perhaps Oppen's most important
working principle in the sense that in his grasping for ade-
quate language, a sense of existence, of personal and social
drama, is defined against the counterfoil of conventional or
unthoughtful language, which may offer solace or benumb,
but which, in effect, distances the individual from what is ac-
tually happening. In the main sequence of *Seascape: Needle's
Eye* entitled "Some San Francisco Poems," there is a constant
play between these modes of language. The first poem in the
series describes the mass migration of young people to a rock
concert, yet

> the songs they go to hear on
> this occasion are no one's own . . . [32]

"No one's own" points at the illusionary nature of this mystical
and ephemeral feeling of togetherness on the part of the young,
a mystique which Oppen does not regard as their sole prop-
erty (though, there, it has special importance for Oppen). For
Oppen, such mysticism is a fiction compounded out of the
emotional reality of human longings and feelings of isola-
tion—feelings which are easily exploitable (one thinks of na-
tionalistic and cultural versions of such exploitation). These

feelings, Oppen maintains, must be understood and exposed if revolutions and reforms are not to be the series of mistaken movements that they have been.

On the level of language, Oppen seems to call into question the entire enterprise of symbol-making. He examines its childhood roots, where

> Night hums like the telephone dial tone blue gauze
> Of the forge flames the pulse
> Of infant
> Sorrows at the crux[33]

Oppen sees this "crux" as the intersection of emotion and the imaginary object it creates to bind it. Thus, the poem continues, "the elves the / Magic people in their world / Among the plant roots," are the latent content, as Freud might say, of superstitions and mystiques: they represent

> hopes
> Which are the hopes
>
> Of small self interest called
>
> Superstition chitinous
> Toys of the children wings
> Of the wasp.
>   (from "The Occurrences," *Collected Poems*)[34]

That these are, to Oppen, subtly dangerous creations seems implied in that final image of the wasp wings. To live by them leads again to recurrent social failure. Such failure has already been implied in the first poem of the series.

> as the tremendous volume of the music takes
> over obscured by their long hair they seem
> to be mourning.[35]

What is manifest here, as in Oppen's earlier work, is a rather important and profound ambivalence toward the creative faculty itself, a faculty which in its power to symbolize and to create empathy towards various conceptions of reality is not without its formal, social and political dangers. For, while it may be true that imagination itself cannot be denied, it can be, in Oppen's opinion, frustrated and misapplied. Oppen would have us believe that there is no morality per se in the creative life—this perhaps goes against the notion of the artist as *savant* or *enfant terrible* leading us on to spiritual heights. In Oppen, there is only a curious kind of moral possibility within the creative act. He puts this quite bluntly in "Five Poems about Poetry" in *This In Which* (1965).

> Art
> Also is not good
>
> For us
> Unless like the fool
>
> Persisting
> In his folly
>
> It may rescue us
> As only the true
>
> Might rescue us . . . [36]

For Oppen, this moral possibility lies in the artist's fidelity to that Heideggerian world of appearance and to a language which seeks to make, as he said in his essay "The Mind's Own Place" (*Kulchur Magazine*, 1963), "clear pictures of the world in verse which mean to be clear, to be honest, to produce the realization of reality, and to construct a form out of no desire for the trick of gracefulness, but in order to make it possible to grasp, to hold the insight which is the content of the poem."[37]

We have in Oppen's oeuvre a body of work the protagonist of which is language struggling with the clichéd and unthoughtful language of mass mind and mass fantasy. The artist's attempt to give voice to the visible world becomes a form of *claritas*, offering out the possibility of an intersubjective reality, that is, one in which there will be some occasions in which human beings agree and which, as a result, are provisionally "true." If in Oppen's poetry language is transformed, it would seem to be from individuated literal words into a kind of supraliteralism consisting of statements which, as Oppen puts it, "cannot not be understood." The mystery of such statements would lie not in their need to be explained, but in the sheer substance of their existence. They would be that "other miracle" which the French philosopher Merleau-Ponty refers to in saying: "It is easy to strip language and action of all meaning and make them seem absurd. . . . But that other miracle, the fact that in an absurd world language and behavior do have meaning for those who speak and act, remains to be understood."*

Intensity of sight, its literal counterpart in language, and the clarity in effect which these become are the essential modes in Oppen's work by which reality is grasped. An attitude, an impression, even the deepest expression of an emotion, is rendered in terms of the visible. As a modality, sight and transformation, through the means of vision—almost in the manner of Donne and the Metaphysicals—are the agents of love, singular and personal love. Thus, in "A Morality Play: Preface" from *Seascape: Needle's Eye*, light is played upon as a sort of metaphor of interanimation, not unlike the function of sight in "The Ecstasy."

> Never to forget her naked eyes
>
> Beautiful and brave
> Her naked eyes
>
> Turn inward
>
> Feminine light
>
> The unimagined
> Feminine light

*Maurice Merleau-Ponty, quoted in the translator's introduction to *Sense and Non-Sense* by Maurice Merleau-Ponty, p. xvi.

> Feminine ardor
>
> Pierced and touched[38]

Here, as with "the commonplace that pierces or erodes," love
and the visible are intertwined, bridging individual lives. The
morality play of the title lies in the distinction between this
personal sense of love and the abstract uses of the word, a
juxtaposition which is the development of a theme previously
elaborated in "Of Being Numerous" (1968), where the indi-
vidual, in his isolation both mentally and physically, the "ship-
wreck of the singular," is transcended not through any abstrac-
tion of "humanity," but through attentiveness and curiosity, a
form of love of the visible. Without this attentiveness, ex-
pressed in "Morality Play" even "tho all say / Huddled among
each other / Love," there is only the implicit continuous failure
of mankind *en masse*, the apocalyptic image.

> This city died young
> You too will be shown this
> You will see the young people
> Leaving again in rags[39]

As Dembo's essay suggests, this love within clarity or as a
form of clarity is, for Oppen, the central impulse which re-
solves the dialectic of seeing and naming, an experience very
much akin to the philosopher's sense of wonder.

> It is impossible the world should be either good or bad
> If its colors are beautiful or if they are not beautiful
> If parts of it taste good or if no parts of it taste good
> It is as remarkable in one case as the other
> (from "And Their Winters and Nights in
> Disguise," *Collected Poems*)[40]

Taken this way, clarity itself is a good which transcends *and*
thereby tests our ordinary systems of value. Oppen stresses
this point throughout his work, as in "Route" (one of the poems
in *Of Being Numerous*):

Imagine a man in the ditch
The wheels of the overturned wreck
Still spinning—

I don't mean he despairs, I mean if he does not
He sees in the manner of poetry.[41]

If we recall that the poet's truth is encountered at the "outer limits of the ego," such clarity becomes a way of bearing witness which is neither academic nor detached; for all of its relation to philosophy, Oppen's poetry has left the ivory tower and gone among men and things, both intellectually and emotionally. Thus, in "And Their Winters and Their Nights in Disguise," the world's remarkableness is tempered by the suffering of men (as in war), for

. . . against this
We have suffered fear, we know something of fear
And of humiliation mounting to horror . . .[42]

Yet it is the uniqueness and power of Oppen's work not to leave the matter resting there as another image of social horror. Rather, he explores further the ambivalence of bearing witness (another dimension of his ambivalent relation to creativity), suggesting that in seeking out the truth, the poet is also obliged to forbear the schizophrenic and vicarious glorifications of both terrors and heroics. Thus, the foxholes of the poem are "*these little dumps* / the poem is about them," and a terrible fascination lies in the fact that "our hearts are twisted / In dead men's pride." As with other images of mass mind and fantasy, Oppen insists that it is not truth but falseness, mystical falseness, which makes an adventure out of these horrors, which makes them both endangering and attractive to the imagination.

Minds may crack

But not for what is discovered

Unless that everyone knew
And kept silent

> Our minds are split
> To seek the danger out
>
> From among the miserable soldiers[43]

By virtue of the poet's ambivalence, the truths that Oppen discovers and gives voice to remain partial and speculative, fragile as the shifts of sight and life itself. However, it must also be said that Oppen's skepticism seems often more alive to possibility than to the comforting voice of wisdom. For it is the depth of Oppen's work, the level at which he seeks for answers, that makes his skepticism never an exercise, never the hubris of a sophist. Indeed, this poet's search for clarity, "the needle's eye" in the title of the book, ultimately becomes, for the poet, a way into the praise of the world.

> . . . conviction's
>
> Net of branches
> In the horde of events the sacred swarm avalanche
>
> Masked in the sunset
>
> Needle after needle more numerous than planets
>
> Or the liquid waves
> In the tide rips
>
> We believe   we believe
> (# 6 of "Some San Francisco Poems," *Collected Poems*)[44]

Oppen is unique in American poetry. While he has marked out for himself the burden of the singular, the isolate man, that both more than and less than Romantic hero of the Western drama of the mind, the one who, in rending the veil, finds another and yet another before him, he has never taken the fashionable position of being "alienated" or messianic. The few commentators on his work have noted his capacity to remain free of redemptive and prescriptive attitudes, to remain at once free and skeptical, even with regard to his own efforts (note the question mark in the first line below):

> We address the future?
>
> Unsure of the times
> Unsure I can answer
>
> In wrath we await
>
> The rare poetic
> of veracity . . .[45]

Yet there is an aspect of Oppen's work which keeps it continually positive and human—human in the sense that it aligns itself with a belief in the value of an ongoing poetic process, in particular the process of exploring reality through a creative effort. There is, for example, the recognition of that impulse which transcends one's personal death, as in the following passage from the earliest of Oppen's mature work ("Image of the Engine," *The Materials*, 1962):

> Endlessly, endlessly
> The definition of mortality
>
> The image of the engine
>
> That stops.
> We cannot live on that.
> I know that no one would live out
> Thirty years, fifty years, if the world were ending
>
> With his life.[46]

This poem implicitly acknowledges the existence of a community in which the poet's labor both weighs and expresses, through language, the feeling of shared experience; perhaps, in Oppen's case that only occurs at that point where "it cannot not be understood." In *Seascape: Needle's Eye*, there is an almost elegiac sense of the transmittal of the poet's burden to the young, to the children, who, so Oppen claims, will become "new skilled fishermen / In the great bays and narrow bights."[47] It is these children, Oppen tells us, who will find that

> In the continual sound
> Are chords
> Not yet struck
> Which will be struck
> Nevertheless yes[48]

Against the songs which are "no one's own," Oppen has raised the prospect of lives realized in authentic language, in language bearing the weight of the visible as evidence of its attempt to be clearly understood. The nearly ringing "Nevertheless yes" would seem to declaim a compensatory possibility, the continual recurrence of poetic speech. The last lines of *Seascape: Needle's Eye* locate this recurrence in the young. Oppen sums it up in "Exodus":

> We dreamed to each other
> Miracle of the children
> The brilliant children   Miracle
>
> Of their brilliance   Miracle
>
> Of[49]

It is this possibility of recurrence which illuminates the populist strain running throughout the poems of Oppen's most recent work, *Primitive*. The poems of the book, even as they are charged (as befits a man writing in his seventies) with the meaning of being a poet, are also an attempt to come to terms with America, to elaborate and show forth an almost Whitmanesque faith in the earlier sources of his poetry: the ordinary working people he encountered, and the young. The resulting work, while stylistically close to *Seascape: Neele's Eye*, contains perhaps Oppen's most public and visionary poetry. The poems, in their moving companionship with others, echo Whitman's transpersonal concerns.

> . . . I am
> of that people the grass
>
> blades touch

and touch in their small

distances the poem
begins[50]

Such poetry is at once celebratory and elegiac; even as it affirms kinship ("I dreamed myself of their people . . . "), it probes the great sense of loss one finds in the American people, speaking of something failed or incomplete, reminding us of how many of Whitman's hopes remain unfulfilled.

The lines of poetry in *Primitive* are intense, painful, and declamatory and have that unique tone which is one of Oppen's major contributions to our poetry.

> . . . young workmen's
> loneliness on the structures has touched
> and touched the heavy tools   tools
> in our hands in the clamorous
> country birth-
> light savage
> light of the landscape.[51]

In these two late books, *Seascape: Needle's Eye* and *Primitive*, Oppen has created from the concerns of his earlier work, a sustained and moving poetry, one that is as important as it is distinctive. In an age of false gods and false certainties, Oppen's intention to mean, to seek clarity, transcends our usual notions of a poetics, for in its detailed richness both history and present seem to be served. As Oppen notes in *Primitive*, harking back to the very beginning of his career and his insistence on the visual, "the tongues of appearance / speak in the unchosen journey . . . the words out of that whirlwind his."[52] In Oppen, this "unchosen journey" has been transformed into a powerful poetry of both collective and individual pain and loss, into a desire, as he puts it in the last lines of *Primitive*, to make "a music more powerful," a music meant to redeem humanity "till other voices wake us or we drown."[53]

Such a poetry becomes the voice of our deepest feeling and doubts, upholding, in the face of death and aging, the value of the voice itself at its most unbearably beautiful and poignant moments—perhaps no more so than in this poem to Mary Oppen, the poet's wife:

> How shall we say how this happened, these stories, our stories
>
> Scope, mere size, a kind of redemption
> Exposed still and jagged on the San Francisco hills
>
> Time and depth before us, paradise of the real, we
>   know what it is
>
> To find now depth, not time, since we cannot, but depth
>
> To come out safe   to end well
>
> We have begun to say goodbye
> To each other
> And cannot say it

("Anniversary Poem," Collected Poems)[54]

I think that Oppen has tried to do nothing more than to make our condition absolutely clear. It is a major achievement. Oppen stands alone in that his poetry is not composed of the effects of modern life upon the self, but is rather our most profound investigation of it.

8 The Objectivist Tradition: Some Further Considerations

George Oppen states in the opening passage of *Of Being Numerous*:

> There are things
> We live among 'and to see them
> Is to know ourselves.'[1]

Among "things" we live with, see, and come to know ourselves by are the poems of our time. For poetry, Heidegger reminds us, is an act which founds whole historical worlds. An Objectivist poetry, involving a poetics more or less subscribed to by a group of poets labeled Objectivists, who were in constant contact with each other over three or four decades, founds its Heideggerian historical worlds in "rested totality," Zukofsky might claim, in sincerities and objectifications as fields of possibility rather than in strictures on form. For we live in an age, Zukofsky tells us, "that will not bear too regular a form," an age saturated with the revolutionary thought of Einstein and Heisenberg pressing at our backs, an age in which our Nietzschean "eternal recurrences" manifest themselves as variations on an as-yet-to-be-revealed theme. Poetry in such a time is the music of indeterminacy; George Lukacs warns us in *Soul and Form* that it now "consists of the dominance of the accompaniment over the solo voice."[2] Poems and poetries no longer successfully enter into our lives as wisdom, as they did in the nineteenth century, but as occasions and registrations of being wise or unwise, lucky or unlucky, within time and event. Our poems require a resemblance to instantaneously gathered *sensibilia*, contradictory and competing gestalts, perspectives, apprehensions in time. They seek to express what D. H. Lawrence called "poetry of that which is at hand: the immediate present." Judgment has a lighter hand in these matters.

And therefore, we are right to conjure the contemporary poet nearly as a kind of relativist, operating within a field of relations, a relativist, that is, until the poem finds its moment of closure and the absolute of "this is what it meant to me" is pronounced. And how different is this absolute from the wisdom-dispensing poems of the past, from the hectoring urge of moral applicability.

With Aristotle, then, we may conjecture that a distinction exists between the orderings of the historian or scientist and those of the poet. But this too is no longer the simple case of being subject to different laws and different mental operations. Rather, what we must say of the poem, finally, is that it is subject to different intentions. For if the historian's or scientist's world is an arrangement, an ordering with "order" in mind, i.e., something of a *fait accompli*, an articulated design, the "historical" world founded by the poem is a gratuitous array, a mixed field of forces across the human disciplines, a product of the poet's willing entrance or submission to the world and to its mutually compelling systems of thought. It seeks out, again in Lawrence's words, "the pure relationship with the living universe." The poem then, to the extent that it is less constrained than the disciplines, is the result of the interaction between the live poet and random or inarticulate promptings of both world and language. The poem, in this sense, is before the fact, created by virtue of a methodological difference with other forms of knowledge.

This difference is explored and lived through, in one way or another, with the Objectivist poets. Oppen, for example, claims in *Notes on Prosody?* that "the poem is NOT built out of words, one cannot make a poem by sticking words into it, it is the poem which makes the words and contains their meaning."[3] Where then is the representation, the "thing" (the scientific formula or history's image of an age) to be represented? If we follow Oppen, what we seem to arrive at is a new compact between poet and poem, not new as an invention perhaps but as a discovery; for the Objectivist poem does not enact a mimesis but mediates between representational systems. It is subject, like the King's subject, to thought; it is, to modify Heidegger's influential phrase, the clearing house of other knowledge. Objectivist practice would seem to be a constant shunning of any systematic ethos; having fallen under the sway of our newest understandings, it is part of what Géfin calls, in *Ideogram*, "the accurate artistic expression of this posthumanist reality."[4] The Objectivist poem lacks the soundingboards of even our recent poetic past, the agrarian backtracking of the Fugitives, for example, or the politicized Anglicanism of Eliot. It foreswears the archaic as an idealized poetic world, thus marking itself off from the works of Olson and the ethnopoetic poets. Yet Objectivist poetry is not at all comfortable with the deterministic Freudianism of so much contemporary domestic poetry either. The Objectivists, and this is a critical if not poetic difficulty, lean into uncertainty. The test qua test of their poetry, applied by the poet, is in this feeling of being on the edge. Oppen sums it up precisely: "When the man writing is frightened by a word, he may have started (writing a poem). . . ."[5] This is to be composing poetry at the horizon of knowledge, never out of touch with thought but at what Heidegger refers to as "the boundary of the boundless."

Objectivist poetry is, therefore, not a thought *about* something but thought itself (language, statement, poem), already "perfect" in the sense Wittgenstein once used the word as a synonym for completed, i.e., something in accordance with Oppen's "that which cannot not be understood."

Zukofsky's procedures may be said to take up this same problem in another way, for Zukofsky's attentiveness is, in a sense, spatial; his poems are a compositional space, a place for the interaction of a multiplicity of thoughts, feelings, and facts, which are, in the poem, continually weighed, checked, and balanced. The poem is not an afterthought concerning these materials, but the very process of their mediation. The English critic Eric Mottram writes of Zukofsky that "his experience is order because the poem articulates it."[6]

Out of such "order" come new possibilities of knowledge. Just such a point and its concomitant implications are developed by William Carlos Williams in his *Embodiment of Knowledge*. And Aristotle's denigration of history, that is, "poetry is graver," before the poet's workings seems to involve a similar consideration.

Objectivist poetry, in the argument I am constructing here, is, first of all, a test of other articulations, of other lingual expressions. And since it is not *a priori* thought out in the realm of other discourses, its issuance, when laid alongside other discourse, is violent and creative. For, like all significant poetry, Objectivist poetry is an uncertain element, a slightly foreign body, brought into relation with existing world-views, knowledge and other poetries. Its perturbation with respect to other thought, its disturbance in the data-bank, is two-fold: not only will the poem, non-conforming as it is, be difficult to categorize or rationalize, but the knowledge, which may be said to radiate from it once it is taken up as both literary artifact and lived occasion, may displace or alter already existing knowledge. Perhaps the only test of poetry in this age of proliferating poets and shrinking numbers of readers, a test surely applicable to the Objectivists, is to consider whether the poem, no matter how self-harmonized its parts, creates disharmony, disquiet, openings or irruptions in conceptual knowledge.

True, this idea, proposing contrasts in the orderings of poetry and science, has its own oddity. For poems, of course, are the conspiratorial intertwinings of man and *logos*; this latter word is used here instead of "word" or "language," as with Heraclitus, to suggest large-scale inspirings or to recount, as the philosopher Hans-Georg Gadamer wishes to remind us, that "our finitude as human beings is encompassed by the infinity of language."[7] The writer (poet) then is not a user of the tool "language" but is a kind of idiom (Merleau-Ponty's formulation) or a genre. And the production of the poet, whose only law is the questioning of his own habit of mind, can be distinguished from that of the scientist because the latter's agenda involves an attempt to rationalize lived experience into law. In Merleau-Ponty's words, "science manipulates things and gives up living in them."[8]

What can be said of science may also be said of conventional notions of the poetic tradition: the typology of canon formation, the classification of authors, and so forth, like the generalizing and abstracting laws of science, present the history of authorship as the history of repertoires of devices and effects. The Objectivist sense of tradition, most clearly enunciated by Zukofsky, is a history not of old or new cookiecutters but of articulated mind-body states, of capacities to "tune in" on the "human tradition." This tradition, a response to felt needs, to "keeping time with the pulse of existence," and not to the representations of the classroom or writing workshop, is what informs an individual poetic talent. We do not stand, as we discover, on Dante's *terza rima*, but on Dante himself.

It is here that the dynamic tension of past-present becomes interesting. For what distinguishes Objectivist work is its sensitivity to the spirit of the tradition as a whole, not to any particular instancing of it. The poet does not choose between techniques, genres, stances, fashions, for such choosing would be self-limiting. Rather, rightness or aptness of craft entails or involves the largest of aspirations since, for the Objectivist, in this case Zukofsky, "the scientific definition of poetry can be based on nothing less than the world, the entire humanly known world." Craft then means an aspiration which would make it possible that "the whole art may appear in one line of the poet or take a whole life's work in which to appear."[9] Thus, Zukofsky, in "An Objective," disassociates himself from the ordinary concepts of taste and canon-making to embrace the largest possible meaning of tradition.

> Only good poetry—good an unnecessary adjective—is contemporary or classical. A standard of taste can be characterized only by acceptance of particular communication and concerned, so to speak, whenever the intelligence is in danger of being cluttered, with exclusions—not with books, but with poetic invention. The nothing, not pure nothing, left over is not a matter of 'recencies', but a matter of *pasts*, maybe *pasties*.
>
> It would be just as well then dealing with 'recencies' to deal with Donne or Shakespeare, if one knew them as well as a linguistic usage not their own can know them.[10]

The informing elements of a new tradition, its particular "recencies," knowledge, a sense of history and the prior traditions of which one is a part, are gathered as a unique occasion of work and thought in the Objectivists. This tradition, as it too becomes visible and so enters into dialogue with our various poetries, is particularly powerful and suggestive. We could call this the tradition's "conviction," its believability not as truth but, as Oppen defines it in "Of Being Numerous," as

> Clarity
>
> In the sense of *transparency*,
> I don't mean that much can be explained.
>
> Clarity in the sense of silence.[11]

The mind is quieted in its peace, in the poem's "rested totality," which, though true to the "science" of poetic tradition, may not amount to much as Science or Reason. Oppen further maintains that the poem seeks to satisfy "not truth but each other." Its form is closer to love than intellectual dominance. Thus, the sense of conviction which it bears emerges not out of the older, human-centered sense of mastery of experience, a kind of humanist arrogance, but out of its show of vulnerability, out of the poet's willingness to enter experience disarmed and to relinquish the dictates or niceties of form when form threatens the sincerity of expression. As in the throes of love, the poet not only breaks with received forms (in this case, of the poem) but with the form of his own mind-set, his self-image as poet. This is not avant-gardism but blunt need or desire for clarity. At the level of the poem, this is a willingness, as Oppen has written, "to refuse the trick of gracefulness."

In this sense, the Objectivists can be said to work against the twin notions of the poem as autonomous object and indeterminate artifact. Objectivist art, both as theory and practice, is an art always *in relation*. The cadence of a Zukofsky or Niedecker poem, for example, its urging to sing or say "out of deep silence," implies not a telegram to or from the void, but a formalized wish to bridge the difficult gap between poem and reader. The poem's tight rhythms, as they animate the reader, interfere with the urge to distance or symbolize the "contents" of the poem. Objectivist poetry, with its leaps of thought and perception, as in Oppen or Rakosi, often requires the reader to "fill in" the gap, to extrapolate or think around the materials of the poem's images. In Reznikoff, the denial of conclusiveness, the desire to be resolutely evidential, opens the space for the reader's judgment or interpretation. The gap or lacuna, the leap across linguistic space, is not simply a flag or marker to indicate how the material of the Objectivist poem is to be read but is, in effect, the arena for discourse and participation. In such a discourse, history is again a form of knowledge and interpretation (an object of knowledge which can be approached) rather than a form of destiny or dictatorial mandate. The Objectivist poem does not aspire to autonomy but

to something closer to the "I—Thou" connection put forth by
Martin Buber: "Primary words do not signify things but they
intimate relations. Primary words do not describe something
that might exist independently of them, but being spoken they
bring about existence.[12] Conviction, then, is a net of branches,
an entangling in music (Zukofsky and Niedecker), or an ex-
pression of lines of sight made lingual (Oppen and Rakosi).
Thus, Objectivist poetry rescues the image from both its liter-
ary theatricality and from its implied status as a datum of sci-
ence by transforming the "out there" into Zukofsky's sense of
"living with things as they exist." Such a poetry adds to sight
the burden or savor of communication, of intersubjectivity, of
words as human arousal (my self, my other).

In Objectivist poetry, Aristotle's vexed views concerning
history and poetry are mediated and in a sense reconciled. The
relationship between history and poetry has always been a
troubling one. The example of Pound, as I have discussed in
the introduction, is useful to contemplate here. According to
Kenner, in his discussion of the Objectivists and Pound in *A
Homemade World*, the "requisite objectification" was present, in
Pound, nearly from the beginning, but the "sincerity," the felt
weight in pain and loss, the cost of historicizing, of Pound's
imagining, appeared only with the *Pisan Cantos*. (This is, of
course, a critical shibboleth, but the cliché has its core of hard
truth.)

Pound, until the *Pisan Cantos*, reorders and displays his-
torical elements until "all ages are contemporaneous," until his
poem "contains history." Objectivist "history," by contrast, is
cumulative, embedded in the meanings behind words and sig-
naled by the cadence or music in which they are embedded;
the poem, not history, is accurately "tuned" as a result of the
poet's knowledge of the historical "association" in the word.
History is less like a lesson than a pressure; as with the termi-
nology of Objectivist poetics, it is meant to translate man for
the present. The backward "golden age-ism," the quest for the
archaic or primordial moment, the Adamic speech act, is con-

spicuous because of its absence in Objectivist poetics. Instead one confronts a present dynamic awareness of historical accretion in which no outcome is assured, no particularized rule, model, or standard is issued by which to live. The contemplation of history, as with Rakosi's contemplation of form, leads ultimately to "the existential world."

Objectivist poetry, it seems, would substitute for the historical lesson a kind of time-bound adeptness. The poet's precise function is in arriving at—not in dictating—some language (the poem) which embodies a skillfulness in apprehending the present. Thus, one can look at Objectivist poetics as honing insight, as refusing the nostalgia of a past time's modality, as ever uncertain.

Ever uncertain. How then are we to understand in the light of this sense of uncertainty, the notion of "rested totality," the ultimate goal or attainment of the Objectivist poem. For "rested totality," we are told by Zukofsky, is synonymous with "the mind's perfect peace." These two terms seem utterly at odds with the sense of uncertainty we have just discussed, and also with the idea that I have developed earlier in this study: that of Objectivist poetry as a peculiarly interactive poetry. The contradiction is significant.

We can perhaps take a clue from George Lukacs' remarks on the notion of "composition" in *Soul and Form*. A "composition," Lukacs tells us, is something "you cannot enter into, you cannot come to terms with it in the usual way. Our relationship to a composition—to something that has already taken form—is clear and unambiguous, even if it is enigmatic and difficult to explain: it is the feeling of being both near and far which comes with great understanding, *that profound sense of union which is yet eternally a being-separate, a standing outside. It is a state of longing*" (my italics).[13] The Objectivist poem, the product of an Objectivist poetics, registers its "rested totality" as an instance of completed form; that is, all its elements and all its exclusions have been accounted for and considered, not only against the weight of tradition but against the weight of our time. In this, it is synonymous with Lukacs' "composition." It engenders longing—and here the poem is nearly a stand-in for its poet—because, like persons, it arouses the attractive possibilities of uncertainty and desire. And like these possibilities, it is ever alive, ever capable of evoking one's creativity, of evoking the deep transformations which are at the center of life and poetic art. In this way, the openness of Zukofsky's poetics, Oppen's and Rakosi's situating of form as a question, and the varied though formal reticences of Reznikoff and Niedecker propose a poetics of workability, a relation to tradition that seems to combine depth and ease and intellectual rigor. This study, then, has come full circle, for the sense of workability is, in itself, an open and unfettered prophecy.

Notes
Selected Bibliography
Index

Notes

Preface

1. Louis Zukofsky, "An Objective," originally printed in *Poetry Magazine* (Chicago, 1931), reprinted in *An "Objectivists" Anthology*, (New York and Var, France: Le Beausset, 1932), collected in *Prepositions: The Collected Critical Essays* (London: Rapp & Carroll, 1967), reprinted in an expanded edition as *Prepositions: The Collected Critical Essays of Louis Zukofsky: Expanded Edition* (Berkeley: Univ. of California Pr., 1981), p. 12. (All references are to the Univ. of California Pr. edition.) This and other essays by Zukofsky in *Prepositions* constitute some of the major statements of Objectivist poetics. In this study, I shall refer to their publication in *Prepositions* although they have been slightly altered and edited from their original form.

2. Zukofsky, quoted in "The 'Objectivist' Poet: Four Interviews," introduced and conducted by L. S. Dembo, *Contemporary Literature* 10 (1969): 204. In this issue, Dembo interviews Zukofsky, George Oppen, Carl Rakosi, and Charles Reznikoff.

3. Mary Oppen, *Meaning A Life* (Santa Barbara: Black Sparrow Pr., 1978), p. 83.

4. Hugh Kenner, *The Pound Era* (Berkeley and Los Angeles: Univ. of California Pr., 1971), p. 406.

1 The Objectivists: Some Discrete Speculations

1. Serge Fauchereau, "Poetry in America: Objectivism," trans. Richard Lebovitz from "Poésie Objectiviste," (*Les Lettres Nouvelles*, 1967), *Ironwood* 6 (1975): 51. "Objectivism" is a term that Zukofsky maintains he never used since it implied too much the name of a movement. He preferred "Objectivist," which seemed to him to refer to some quality of poetry

rather than to an -ism to which poets dogmatically adhered. (See Zukofsky to Dembo, *Contemporary Literature* 10: 203.)

2. Walt Whitman, *Walt Whitman: Complete Poetry and Collected Prose* (New York: The Library of America, 1982), p. 183.

3. Zukofsky, *Prepositions: The Collected Critical Essays of Louis Zukofsky: Expanded Edition* (Berkeley: Univ. of California Pr., 1981), p. 12.

4. George Oppen to Serge Fauchereau, "Three Oppen Letters With A Note," *Ironwood* 5 (1975): 83.

5. Ezra Pound, "Vorticism," *Fortnightly Review* 96 (Sept. 1, 1914): 469.

6. Oppen, *Collected Poems* (New York: New Directions, 1975), p. 80.

7. William Carlos Williams, *Selected Essays* (New York: New Directions, 1954), pp. 105–12.

8. Ibid.

9. Oppen to Dembo, "The 'Objectivist' Poet: Four Interviews," *Contemporary Literature* 10: 163.

10. Zukofsky, *Prepositions*, p. 14.

11. Pound, "A Retrospect," originally published 1913; reprinted in *The Literary Essays of Ezra Pound*, ed. T. S. Eliot (New York: New Directions, 1954), p. 5.

12. Laszlo Géfin, *Ideogram: History of a Poetic Method* (Austin: Univ. of Texas Pr., 1982), p. xvii. Géfin's book is an excellent study of the influence of Pound's poetics upon contemporary American poetry. Like Fauchereau, Géfin sees ideogrammatic and Objectivist poetics as especially important and fruitful modalities by which a diverse group of poets encounter and articulate contemporary experience in the light of new understandings in science, art, and philosophy.

13. Pound makes use of the term "luminous detail" throughout his theorizing on poetry to suggest a historical datum which reveals the character and psychological make-up of an age. His "gists" and "piths" and his use of the term "vortex" as "an intellectual and emotional complex in a moment of time" are nearly synonymous with "luminous detail" in that they all suggest a unique knotting or gathering from which a historical epoch can be intuited.

14. Géfin, *Ideogram*, p. xii.

15. Zukofsky, *Prepositions*, p. 15.

16. Ibid.

17. Oppen, "The 'Objectivist' Poet: Four Interviews," p. 161.

18. Oppen in an unpublished letter to Michael Heller.

19. Rachel DuPlessis, "Objectivist Poetics and Political Vision: A Study of Oppen and Pound," *George Oppen: Man and Poet*, ed. Burton Hatlen (Orono, Maine: The National Poetry Foundation, 1981), p. 145. DuPlessis's essay is a remarkable untangling of Poundian and Objectivist poetics, an extremely sophisticated argument for viewing Oppen's po-

etics in particular, but also the Objectivists' as a whole, as distinctly different from Pound's.

20. Zukofsky, *Prepositions*, p. 167.

21. Ibid.

22. Zukofsky, *Bottom: On Shakespeare* (Austin: The Ark Pr., 1965), p. 39.

23. Ibid., p. 251.

24. Carl Rakosi, *Ex Cranium, Night* (Los Angeles: Black Sparrow Pr., 1975), p. 161.

25. Maurice Merleau-Ponty, *The Phenomenology of Perception*, trans. Colin Smith (London: Routledge & Kegan Paul, 1962), p. 53.

26. Oppen, *Collected Poems*, p. 140.

27. Ibid., p. 217.

28. Oppen, "Three Oppen Letters," p. 84.

29. Robert Lowell, "Eye and Tooth," *For the Union Dead* (New York: Farrar, 1964), pp. 18–19.

30. Hugh Kenner, *A Homemade World* (New York: Morrow, 1975), p. 187.

31. Charles Baudelaire, *My Heart Laid Bare*, ed. with an introduction by Peter Quennell; trans. Norman Cameron (London: George Weidenfeld & Nicolson, 1950), p. 195.

32. William Butler Yeats, *Selected Poems and Two Plays of William Butler Yeats*, ed. M. L. Rosenthal (New York: MacMillan, 1962), p. 95.

33. Whitman, *Complete Poetry and Collected Prose*, p. 46.

34. Zukofsky, *Prepositions*, p. 14.

35. Oppen, "The 'Objectivist' Poet: Four Interviews," p. 173.

36. Oppen, *Collected Poems*, p. 172.

37. Kenner, *A Homemade World*, p. 187.

38. Oppen, *Collected Poems*, pp. 166–67.

2 Louis Zukofsky's Objectivist Poetics: Reflections and Extensions

1. Zukofsky, *Prepositions*, pp. 12–13.

2. Ibid., p. 12.

3. Zukofsky, *All: The Collected Short Poems, 1923–1964* (New York: Norton, 1971), p. 75.

4. Ibid., p. 78.

5. Ibid., p. 76.

6. Zukofsky, *Prepositions*, p. 20.

7. Zukofsky, *All*, p. 78.

8. Zukofsky, *Prepositions*, p. 15.

3 The Poetry of Louis Zukofsky: To Draw Speech

1. Zukofsky, *A* (Berkeley: Univ. of California Pr., 1978), p. 124.

2. Kenner, on the jacket of *All*.

3. Harold Schimmel, "Zuk. Yehoash David Rex," *Louis Zukofsky: Man and*

Poet, ed. Carroll F. Terrell (Orono, Maine: National Poetry Foundation, 1979), p. 235.

4. Zukofsky, *A Test of Poetry* (New York: Jargon/Corinth Books, 1964), p. vii.

5. Donald Byrd, "The Shape of Zukofsky's Canon," *Louis Zukofsky: Man and Poet*, ed. Carroll F. Terrell (Orono, Maine: National Poetry Foundation, 1979), pp. 163–85.

6. Zukofsky, "Discarded Poems," *Louis Zukofsky: Man and Poet*, ed. Carroll F. Terrell (New York: National Poetry Foundation, 1979), p. 155.

7. Zukofsky, *Prepositions*, pp. 19–23.

8. Zukofsky, *A*, p. 126.

9. Zukofsky, *Prepositions*, p. 18.

10. Ibid., p. 19.

11. Zukofsky, *A*, p. 138.

12. Zukofsky, *Prepositions*, p. 14.

13. Ibid.

14. Ibid., p. 15.

15. Zukofsky, *A*, p. 126.

16. Ibid., pp. 234–35.

17. Zukofsky, *Prepositions*, p. 7.

18. Zukofsky, *A*, p. 128.

19. Ibid., pp. 131 and 156.

20. Zukofsky, *Prepositions*, p. 8.

21. Zukofsky, *Bottom: On Shakespeare*, p. 91. How important the notion of "communication" is to Zukofsky can be seen in the completed quote which reads "The constant of Shakespeare's expression . . . is its inexpressible *trust of expression*, the incentive and end of which is to unite others in friendship. Otherwise there is never any *need* for expression."

22. Merleau-Ponty, *The Phenomenology of Perception*, p. 57.

23. Zukofsky, *A*, p. 127.

24. Ibid., p. 124.

25. Ibid., p. 189.

26. Ibid., pp. 135–36.

27. Ibid., p. 131.

28. Zukofsky, *Prepositions*, p. 23.

29. Zukofsky, *A*, p. 197.

4 Carl Rakosi: Profoundly In Between

1. Rakosi, *Ex Cranium, Night*, p. 103.

2. Ibid., p. 51.

3. Ibid., p. 157.

4. Ibid., p. 118.

5. Rakosi, *Amulet* (New York: New Directions, 1967), p. 56.

6. Walter Benjamin, "On Some Motifs in Baudelaire," *Illuminations*, trans. Harry Zohn (New York: Schocken Books, 1969), pp. 155–94. The notion of "aura" is specifically discussed in sec. 11, p. 186. There, Benjamin remarks: "Experience of the aura thus rests on the transposition of a response common in human relationships to the relationship between the inanimate or natural object and man. . . . To perceive the aura of an object we look at means to invest it with the ability to look at us in return."

7. Rakosi, *Amulet*, p. 63.

8. Rakosi, *Ex Cranium, Night*, p. 13.

9. Ibid., p. 117.

10. Rakosi, *Amulet*, p. 32.

11. Rakosi, *Ex Cranium, Night*, p. 174.

12. Ibid., p. 161.

13. Rakosi, *Amulet*, p. 14.

14. Rakosi, *Ex Cranium, Night*, p. 23.

15. Ibid., p. 150.

16. Ibid., p. 70.

5 Lorine Niedecker: Light and Silence

1. Lorine Niedecker, "Wintergreen Ridge," *Caterpillar* 3/4 (1968): 234.

2. Zukofsky, *Prepositions*, p. 23.

3. Niedecker, *T & G: The Collected Poems (1936–1966)* (Penland, North Carolina: The Jargon Society, 1968), unpaginated.

4. Ibid.

5. Ibid.

6. Ibid.

7. Lorine Niedecker to Cid Corman, "With Lorine," *Chicago Review* 25, no. 3 (1973).

8. Niedecker, *Caterpillar* 3/4: 229.

9. Niedecker, *T & G*.

10. Ibid.

11. Niedecker to Corman, "With Lorine."

12. Niedecker, *T & G*.

13. Ibid.

14. Ibid.

15. Ibid.

16. Ibid.

17. Ibid.

6 The Modernity of Charles Reznikoff

1. Aristotle's comment in *Rhetoric, Book III* reads: "Nevertheless, these things [matters of style] are of consequence, as I have said, because of the

depravity of the audience." Aristotle, *On Poetry and Style*, trans. G. M. A. Grube (New York: The Liberal Arts Pr., 1958), p. 67.

2. Charles Reznikoff, *The Complete Poems* ed. Seamus Cooney (Santa Barbara: Black Sparrow Pr., 1977), vol. 2, p. 137. This is a two-volume edition of Reznikoff's poems, vol. 1 covering the years 1918–1936, vol. 2, 1937–1975.

3. Reznikoff, *By the Well of Living and Seeing*, ed. Seamus Cooney (Los Angeles: Black Sparrow Pr., 1974). This is a one-volume selection from all of Reznikoff's poems.), p. 38.

4. Ibid. p. 147.

5. Reznikoff, *The Complete Poems* 1:60.

6. Ibid. 2:26.

7. Ibid. 1:72

8. Ibid. 1:127.

9. Ibid. 2:168.

10. Ibid. 1:22.

11. Ibid. 2:94.

12. Ibid. 1:115.

13. Ibid. 1:121.

14. Ibid. 2:191.

15. Reznikoff, *First, There Is the Need*, published as *Sparrow* 52 (Santa Barbara: Black Sparrow Pr., 1977), unpaginated.

16. Reznikoff, *The Complete Poems* 1:158.

17. Ibid. 1:182.

7 *The Mind of George Oppen: Conviction's Net of Branches*

1. Oppen, *Collected Poems*, p. 202.

2. Ibid., p. 225.

3. Ibid., p. 24.

4. Oppen, "Three Oppen Letters," p. 84.

5. Oppen, *Collected Poems*, p. 93.

6. Erich Heller, *The Disinherited Mind* (New York: Meridian Book, 1959), p. 267.

7. Oppen, *Collected Poems*, p. 213.

8. Kenner, *The Pound Era*, p. 404.

9. Oppen, *Collected Poems*, p. 6.

10. Ibid., p. 106.

11. Ibid., p. 235.

12. Ibid., p. 26.

13. Ibid., p. 68.

14. Ibid., p. 140.

15. Ibid., p. 97.

16. Ibid., p. 119–20.

17. Ibid., p. 84.
18. Ibid., p. 147.
19. Ibid., p. 148.
20. Ibid., p. 151.
21. Ibid., p. 159.
22. Ibid., pp. 165–66.
23. Ibid., p. 168.
24. Ibid., p. 170–71.
25. Ibid., p. 173.
26. Ibid., p. 174.
27. Ibid., p. 179.
28. Ibid., p. 173.
29. Ibid., p. 206.
30. Ibid., p. 205.
31. Ibid.
32. Ibid., p. 214.
33. Ibid., p. 206.
34. Ibid.
35. Ibid., p. 214.
36. Ibid., p. 84.
37. Oppen, "The Mind's Own Place," *Kulchur 10* (Summer 1963): 2.
38. Oppen, *Collected Poems*, p. 215.
39. Ibid., p. 216.
40. Ibid., p. 217.
41. Ibid., p. 191.
42. Ibid., pp. 217–18.
43. Ibid., p. 218.
44. Ibid., p. 223.
45. Ibid., p. 208.
46. Ibid., p. 19.
47. Ibid., p. 209.
48. Ibid., p. 223.
49. Ibid., p. 229.
50. Oppen, *Primitive* (Santa Barbara: Black Sparrow Pr., 1978), p. 25.
51. Ibid., p. 22.
52. Ibid., p. 19.
53. Ibid., p. 31.
54. Oppen, *Collected Poems*, pp. 219–20.

8 The Objectivist Tradition: Some Further Considerations
1. Oppen, *Collected Poems*, p. 147.
2. George Lukacs, *Soul and Form*, trans. Anne Bostock (Cambridge, Mass.: MIT Pr., 1971), p. 85.

3. Oppen, "Notes on Prosody?", *Ironwood* 5 (1975), back cover.
4. Géfin, *Ideogram*, p. 137.
5. Oppen, *Ironwood* 5 (1975), back cover.
6. Eric Mottram, "1924–1951: Politics and Form in Zukofsky," *Maps* 5 (1973): 76.
7. Hans-Georg Gadamer, *Philosophical Hermeneutics*, trans. and ed. David E. Linge (Berkeley: Univ. of California Pr., 1977), p. 67.
8. Maurice Merleau-Ponty, *The Primacy of Perception*, trans. James M. Edie (Evanston, Ill.: Northwestern Univ. Pr., 1964), p. 159.
9. Zukofsky, *Prepositions*, p. 9.
10. Ibid., p. 16.
11. Oppen, *Collected Poems*, p. 162.
12. Martin Buber, *I and Thou*, trans. Ronald Gregor Smith; 2nd ed. (New York: Charles Scribner's Sons, 1958), p. 3.
13. Lukacs, *Soul and Form*, pp. 91–92.

The Objectivists:
A Selected Bibliography

PRIMARY SOURCES

Lorine Niedecker
New Goose. Prairie City, Ill.: James A. Decker, 1946.
——— *My Friend Tree; Poems*. Edinburgh: Wild Hawthorne Pr., 1961.
——— *North Central*. London: Fulcrum Pr., 1968.
——— *T & G: The Collected Poems (1936–1966)*. Penland, N.C.: The Jargon Society, Penland School, 1968.
——— *My Life By Water: Collected Poems, 1936–1968*. London: Fulcrum Pr., 1968.
"Wintergreen Ridge." *Caterpillar* 3/4 (1968): 229–37.
——— *Blue Chicory*. New Rochelle, N.Y.: Elizabeth Pr., 1976.

George Oppen
Discrete Series. Preface by Ezra Pound. New York: The Objectivist Pr., 1934.
——— *The Materials*. New York: New Directions, 1962.
——— *This In Which*. New York: New Directions, 1965.
——— *Discrete Series*. Cleveland: Asphodel Book Shop, 1966.
——— *Of Being Numerous*. New York: New Directions, 1968.
——— *Alpine: Poems by George Oppen*. Mount Horeb, Wis.: The Perishable Pr., 1969.
——— *Seascape: Needle's Eye*. Fremont, Mich.: Sumac Pr., 1972.
——— *Collected Poems of George Oppen*. London: Fulcrum Pr., 1975.

————— *The Collected Poems of George Oppen.* New York: New Directions, 1975.

————— *Primitive.* Santa Barbara: Black Sparrow Pr., 1978.

Carl Rakosi

————— "Good Prose." *The New Act* 2 (June 1933).

————— *Two Poems.* New York: Modern Editions Pr., 1933. [*The Poetry Scene.*Pamphlet 7.]

————— "The Poem: National Winter Garden Shamrock." *The New Act* 3 (April 1934).

————— *Selected Poems by Carl Rakosi.* Norfolk, Conn.: New Directions, 1941.

————— *Amulet.* New York: New Directions, 1967.

————— *Ere-Voice.* New York: New Directions, 1971.

————— *Ex Cranium, Night.* Los Angeles: Black Sparrow Pr., 1975.

————— *Spiritus, I.* Durham, England: Pig Pr., 1983.

Charles Reznikoff

Rhythms. Brooklyn, N.Y.: De Vinne Pr., 1918.

————— *Rhythms II.* Brooklyn, N.Y.: De Vinne Pr., 1919.

————— *Poems.* New York: Charles Reznikoff, 1920.

————— *Uriel Acosta: A Play and a Fourth Group of Verse.* New York: Cooper Pr., 1921.

————— *Chatterton, The Black Death, and Merriwether Lewis; Three Plays.* New York: The Sunwise Turn, 1922.

————— *Coral, and Captive Israel; Two Plays.* New York: The Sunwise Pr., 1923.

————— *The Black Death; A Play. Menorah Journal* 10 (1924).

————— *Uriel Acosta; A Play. Menorah Journal* 11 (1925).

————— *Five Groups of Verse.* New York: Charles Reznikoff, 1927.

————— *Nine Plays.* New York: Charles Reznikoff, 1927.

————— *By the Waters of Manhattan: An Annual (including Editing and Glosses).* New York: Charles Reznikoff, 1929.

————— *By the Waters of Manhattan.* Introduction by Louis Untermeyer. New York: C. Boni, 1930.

————— *In Memoriam: 1933.* New York: The Objectivist Pr., 1934.

————— *Jerusalem the Golden.* New York: The Objectivist Pr., 1934.

————— *Testimony.* Introduction by Kenneth Burke. New York: The Objectivist Pr., 1934.

Nathan Reznikoff. *Early History of a Sewing Machine Operator.* New York: Charles Reznikoff, 1936. [This is the second part of a family chronicle the first part of which was published as the first part of *By the Waters of Manhattan.*]

————— *Separate Ways.* New York: The Objectivist Pr., 1936.

————— *Going To and Fro and Walking Up and Down.* New York: Futuro Pr. Inc., 1941.

Uriah Z. Engelman. *The Jews of Charleston; A History of an American Jewish Community.* Philadelphia: Jewish Publication Society, 1944.

—— *The Lionhearted; A Story about Jews in Medieval England.* Philadelphia: Jewish Publication Society, 1944.

—— "New Haven: The Jewish Community; Portrait Sketch." *Commentary* 4, no. 5 (November 1947).

—— *Inscriptions: 1944–1956.* New York: Charles Reznikoff, 1959.

—— *Stories and Fantasies from the Jewish Past.* Philadelphia: Jewish Publication Society, 1961.

Louis Marshall, Champion of Liberty: Selected Papers and Addresses Edited by Charles Reznikoff. Philadelphia: Jewish Publication Society, 1961.

—— *By the Waters of Manhattan: Selected Verse.* New York: New Directions, 1962.

Sarah Reznikoff, and Nathan Reznikoff. *Family Chronicle: Early History of a Seamstress (By S. Reznikoff), Early History of a Sewing-Machine Operator (by N. Reznikoff), Needle Trade (by C. Reznikoff).* New York: Charles Reznikoff, 1963.

—— *Testimony: The United States, 1885–1890, Recitative.* New York: New Directions, 1965.

—— *Family Chronicle.* London: N. Bailey with the Human Constitution, 1969.

—— *Needle Trade. In Family Chronicle.* New York: Universe Books, 1971.

—— *By the Well of Living and Seeing: New and Selected Poems 1918–1973.* Edited with an introduction by Seamus Cooney. Los Angeles: Black Sparrow Pr., 1974.

—— *Holocaust.* Los Angeles: Black Sparrow Pr., 1975.

—— *Poems 1918–1936. Volume I of the Complete Poems of Charles Reznikoff.* Edited by Seamus Cooney. Santa Barbara: Black Sparrow Pr., 1976.

—— *The Manner Music.* Introduction by Robert Creeley. Santa Barbara: Black Sparrow Pr., 1977.

—— *Poems 1937–1975. Volume II of the Complete Poems of Charles Reznikoff.* Edited by Seamus Cooney. Santa Barbara: Black Sparrow Pr., 1977.

Louis Zukofsky

—— *An "Objectivists" Anthology.* Edited by Louis Zukofsky. Var, France: Le Beausset, 1932.

—— *Le Style Apollinaire.* Translated by Rene Taupin. Paris: Les Presses Modernes, 1934. Originally published as *The Writings of Guillaume Apollinaire.*

—— *55 Poems.* Prairie City, Ill.: James A. Decker, 1941.

—— *Anew: Poems by Louis Zukofsky.* Prairie City, Ill.: James A. Decker, 1946.

—— *A Test of Poetry.* Brooklyn: The Objectivist Pr., 1948.

——— *Some Time: Short Poems*. (Jargon 15) Stuttgart, Germany: Jonathan Williams, 1956.

——— *Barely and Widely*. Brooklyn: Celia Zukofsky, 1958.

——— *Five Statements for Poetry*. San Francisco: San Francisco State College, 1958.

——— *"A" 1–12*. Ashland, Mass.: Origin Pr., 1959. [With an essay on poetry by the author and a final note by William Carlos Williams.]

——— *It Was*. Kyoto, Japan: Origin Pr., 1961.

——— *"A" 24*. New York: Grossman, 1962.

——— *16 Once Published*. Selected by Celia Zukofsky from *55 Poems, Anew, Some Time, Barely and Widely (1925–1958)*. Edinburgh: Wild Hawthorne Pr., 1962.

——— *Bottom: On Shakespeare*. Austin: Ark Pr. for the Humanities Research Center, Univ. of Texas, 1963.

——— *I's (pronounced "eyes")*. New York: Trobar Pr., 1963.

——— *After I's*. Pittsburgh: Boxwood Pr./Mother Pr., 1964.

——— *Found Objects, 1926–1962*. Georgetown, Ky.: H. B. Chapin, 1964.

——— *A Test of Poetry*. 2d ed. New York: Jargon/Corinth Books, 1964.

——— *"A" Libretto*. New York: Celia Zukofsky, 1965.

——— *All: The Collected Short Poems, 1923–1958*. New York: Norton, 1965.

——— *Finally a Valentine, a Poem*. London: The Piccolo Pr., 1965. ["Opening" #1.]

——— *I sent Thee Late*. Cambridge, Mass.: LHS, 1965.

——— *Iyyob*. London: Turret Books, 1965.

——— *An Unearthing*. Cambridge, Mass.: Harvard Yard Adams House and Lowell House Printers, 1965.

——— *All: The Collected Short Poems, 1956–1964*. New York: Norton, 1966.

——— *"A"–9*. Futura 5. Stuttgart, Germany: Edition Hans Jörg Mayer, 1966. [A broadside.]

——— *"A" 1–12*. London: Jonathan Cape, 1966.

——— *All: The Collected Short Poems, 1923–1958*. London: Jonathan Cape, 1966.

——— *Bottom: On Shakespeare*. Caterpillar 2, Bloomington, Ind., 1966.

——— *A–14*. London: Turret Books, 1967.

——— *"A" 1–12*. Garden City, N.Y.: Doubleday, 1967.

——— *All: The Collected Short Poems, 1956–1964*. London: Jonathan Cape, 1967.

——— *Little: A Fragment for Careenagers*. Los Angeles: Black Sparrow Pr., 1967.

——— *Prepositions: The Collected Critical Essays of Louis Zukofsky*. London: Rapp and Carroll, 1967.

——— *"A"*. Berkeley: Univ. of California Pr., 1968.

——— *80 Flowers*. Luneburg, Vt.: Stinehour Pr., 1968.

——— *Ferdinand, Including It Was.* 2d ed. London: Jonathan Cape, 1968.

——— *Prepositions: The Collected Critical Essays of Louis Zukofsky.* 2nd ed. New York: Horizon Pr., 1968.

——— *"A" 13–21.* Garden City, N.Y.: Doubleday, 1969.

——— *"A" 13–21.* London: Jonathan Cape, 1969.

Celia Zukofsky. *Catullus Fragmenta: A Translation.* London: Turret Books, 1969. [Music by Paul Zukofsky.]

——— *Catullus (Cui Valeri Catulli Veronenisi liber).* London: Cape Goliard Pr., 1969.

——— *The Gas Age.* Newcastle-upon-Tyne, England: Ultima Thule, 1969.

——— *Louis Zukofsky at the American Embassy, London, May 21, 1969.* Newcastle-upon-Tyne, England: Ultima Thule, 1969.

——— *Autobiography.* New York: Grossman, 1970. [Poems set to music by Celia Zukofsky.]

——— *Da A.* Translated by Giovanni Galtieu. Preface by William Carlos Williams. 1st ed. Parma, Italy: Guanda Editore, 1970. [Bilingual presentation of selections from *A, All, Anew.*]

——— *An Era Any Time of Year.* Santa Barbara: Unicorn Pr., 1970.

——— *Initial.* Oblong Octavo Series, no. 12. New York: Ferguson Pr., 1970.

——— *Little: For Careenagers.* New York: Grossman, 1970.

——— *All: The Collected Short Poems, 1923–1964.* New York: Norton, 1971.

——— *Arise, Arise.* 2d ed. New York: Grossman, 1973.

——— *"A" 22 & 23.* New York: Grossman, 1975.

——— *"A".* Berkeley: Univ. of California Pr., 1978.

——— *Prepositions: The Collected Critical Essays of Louis Zukofsky: Expanded Edition.* Berkeley: Univ. of California Pr., 1981.

——— *From "Thanks to the Dictionary".* Buffalo, N.Y.: The Gallery Upstairs. [A single sheet.]

SECONDARY SOURCES

Books and Articles

Aristotle. *On Poetry and Style.* Translated by G. M. A. Grube. New York: The Liberal Arts Pr., 1958.

Baudelaire, Charles. *My Heart Laid Bare.* Edited with an introduction by Peter Quennell. Translated by Norman Cameron. London: George Weidenfeld & Nicolson, 1950.

Benjamin, Walter. *Illuminations.* Translated by Harry Zohn. Introduction by Hannah Arendt. New York: Schocken Books, 1969.

Buber, Martin. *I and Thou.* Translated by Ronald Gregor Smith. 2d ed. New York: Charles Scribner's Sons, 1958.

Fauchereau, Serge. "Poetry in America: Objectivism." Translated by Rich-

ard Lebovitz. *Ironwood* 6 (1975). Originally published as "Poésie Objec-
tiviste." *Les Lettres Nouvelles* (1967).

Gadamer, Hans-Georg. *Philosophical Hermeneutics*. Edited and translated by
David E. Linge. Berkeley: Univ. of California Pr., 1977.

Géfin, Laszlo. *Ideogram: History of a Poetic Method*. Austin: Univ. of Texas Pr.,
1982.

Hatlen, Burton, ed. *George Oppen: Man and Poet*. Orono, Maine: National
Poetry Foundation, 1981.

Heller, Erich. *The Disinherited Mind*. New York: Meridian Book, 1959.

Kenner, Hugh. *A Homemade World*. New York: Morrow, 1975.

—— *The Pound Era*. Berkeley: The Univ. of California Pr., 1971.

Lowell, Robert. *For the Union Dead*. New York: Farrar, 1964.

Lukacs, George. *Soul and Form*. Translated by Anne Bostock. Cambridge,
Mass.: The MIT Pr., 1971.

Mariani, Paul. *William Carlos Williams: A New World Naked*. New York: McGraw-
Hill, 1981.

Merleau-Ponty, Maurice. *The Phenomenology of Perception*. Translated by Colin
Smith. London: Routledge & Kegan Paul, 1962.

——. *The Primacy of Perception*. Translated by James M. Edie. Evanston,
Ill.: Northwestern Univ. Pr., 1964.

Oppen, Mary. *Meaning A Life*. Santa Barbara: Black Sparrow Pr., 1978.

Pound, Ezra. *The Literary Essays of Ezra Pound*. Edited by T. S. Eliot. New
York: New Directions, 1954.

——. "Vorticism." *Fortnightly Review* 96 (September 1, 1914).

Terrell, Carroll F., ed. *Louis Zukofsky: Man and Poet*. Orono, Maine: National
Poetry Foundation, 1979.

Whitman, Walt. *Walt Whitman: Complete Poetry and Collected Prose*. New York:
The Library of America, 1982.

Williams, William Carlos. *Selected Essays*. New York: New Directions, 1954.

Yeats, William Butler. *Selected Poems and Two Plays of William Butler Yeats*.
Edited by M. L. Rosenthal. New York: MacMillan, 1962.

Zukofsky, Celia. *A Bibliography of Louis Zukofsky*. Los Angeles: Black Sparrow
Pr., 1969.

Periodicals
Chicago Review. Vol. 25, no. 3 (1973).
Contemporary Literature. Vol. 10, no. 2 (Spring 1969).
Ironwood 5. Vol. 3, no. 1 (1975).
Kulchur 10. Vol. 3, no. 10 (New York, 1963).
Maps 5. (Shippensberg, Pa., 1973).
Origin 2. 3d ser. (Kyoto, July 1966).
Origin 16. 4th ser. (Boston, July 1981).

Index